pilgrimage of the heart

SATISFY YOUR LONGING FOR ADVENTURE WITH GOD

Blessed are those whose strength is in you,
who have set their hearts on pilgrimage.
(PSALM 84:5)

catherine martin

NAVPRESS

For a free catalog
of NavPress books & Bible studies call
1-800-366-7788 (USA) or 1-800-839-4769 (Canada).
www.NavPress.com

The Navigators is an international Christian organization. Our mission is to advance the gospel of Jesus and His kingdom into the nations through spiritual generations of laborers living and discipling among the lost. We see a vital movement of the gospel, fueled by prevailing prayer, flowing freely through relational networks and out into the nations where workers for the kingdom are next door to everywhere.

NavPress is the publishing ministry of The Navigators. The mission of NavPress is to reach, disciple, and equip people to know Christ and make Him known by publishing life-related materials that are biblically rooted and culturally relevant. Our vision is to stimulate spiritual transformation through every product we publish.

ISBN-13: 978-1-57683-377-3
ISBN-10: 1-57683-377-1

Cover design by David Carlson Design
Cover photo by Douglas E. Walker/Masterfile
Creative Team: Terry Behimer, Karen Lee-Thorp, Amy Spencer, Pat Miller

Some of the anecdotal illustrations in this book are true to life and are included with the permission of the persons involved. All other illustrations are composites of real situations, and any resemblance to people living or dead is coincidental.

Unless otherwise identified, all Scripture quotations in this publication are taken from the HOLY BIBLE: NEW INTERNATIONAL VERSION® (NIV®). Copyright © 1973, 1978, 1984 by International Bible Society. Used by permission of Zondervan Publishing House. All rights reserved. Other versions used include: the *New American Standard Bible* (NASB), © The Lockman Foundation 1960, 1962, 1963, 1968, 1971, 1972, 1973, 1975, 1977, 1995; *The Message: New Testament with Psalms and Proverbs* (MSG) by Eugene H. Peterson, copyright © 1993, 1994, 1995, used by permission of NavPress Publishing Group; the *Williams New Testament* (WMS) by Charles B. Williams, © 1937, 1965, 1966, by Edith S. Williams, Moody Bible Institute of Chicago; the *Holy Bible, New Living Translation*, (NLT) copyright © 1996. Used by permission of Tyndale House Publishers, Inc., Wheaton, Illinois 60189. All rights reserved; and the *Amplified New Testament* (AMP), © The Lockman Foundation 1954, 1958, 1987.

Every effort has been made to locate the owners of copyrighted materials in this publication. Upon notification, the publisher will make proper correction in subsequent printings.

Printed in the United States of America

2 3 4 5 6 7 8 9 10 / 12 11 10 09 08

To my Eternal Companion,
my Lord Jesus Christ,
who has given me a song in the night
and loved me with an everlasting love.

To my earthly companion, my husband, David,
who has loved me deeply and has shared my joys and sorrows
and who is the great love of my life.

To my mother, Elizabeth Stuter Snyder,
who has believed in me
and encouraged me every day of my pilgrimage.

To my dad, Robert Joseph Snyder,
who challenged me to never give up.

To my brother, Robert Joseph Snyder Jr.,
who has shown me what it means to surrender to God
and experience His power in my pilgrimage.

To my mother-in-law, Eloise Maxine Martin,
who has faithfully prayed for me
and loved me as her own daughter.

contents

foreword

We have known Catherine Martin for twenty years, and she has been a close, trusted, and loyal friend. Catherine has a reverence and enthusiasm for God's Word that is refreshing and passionate. Her summa cum laude degree from Bethel Theological Seminary and her experience as an inspirational Christian speaker and Bible study leader enable her to communicate spiritual truth to a vast audience hungering for deeper devotion in their quiet time. *Pilgrimage of the Heart* reflects Catherine's excitement and respect for the Scriptures and will have a tremendous impact on anyone who reads it!

Josh and Dottie McDowell

acknowledgments

Thank you to Dr. Walter Wessel, Dr. Ronald Youngblood, Dr. Al Glenn, Dr. Cliff Anderson, and Dr. Jim Smith, my professors at Bethel Theological Seminary, for encouraging me to work hard and to give my best to the task at hand, and for teaching me how to rightly divide the Word of God.

Thank you to Conni Hudson, who encouraged me to complete this work and led the initial discussions of these quiet times. I never could have written this without you.

Thank you to the faithful women of God who piloted this study before publication: Conni Hudson, Janet Tuerle, Melissa Brown, Sandy Noel, Debra Collins, Linda Osgood, Debbie Griffin, Jane Jeffers, and Leah Phillips. Special thanks to Linda Kelly for piloting this study in Ohio and encouraging me in this project.

Thank you to my family, who has supported me all along the way on this project: David, Mother, Dad, Robert, Tania, Christopher, Kayle, Nana, Eloise, Andy, Ann, Keegan, and James.

Thank you to my newsletter staff—Laurie Bailey, Cay Hough, Maurine Cromwell, and Shirley Peters—for exploring this idea of being God's pilgrim in our issue on pilgrimage.

Special thanks to Andy Kotner, who has been my comrade on this pilgrimage, who has laughed and cried with me, and who has experienced the depths and the heights with me. Thank you for being ever-faithful, dear Andy. Thank you, Thea Dryfhout, for the hours we spent together in the book of Romans and for showing me a very deep love of God. Thank you, Jane Lyons, for being my dear friend and for instant messaging me at just the right time when I was researching on the Internet. Your words and friendship have been a constant source of encouragement to me. Thank you, Paula U'Ren, for sharing the beginnings of Quiet Time Ministries many years ago. Thank you, Shirley Peters, for being such a wonderful example of a woman of God to me.

Thank you to all of the servants of the Lord at NavPress who have so encouraged me in the writing of these books of quiet times: R. Kent Wilson, Dan Rich, Toben Heim, Terry Behimer, and Amy Spencer.

A special thank you to Karen Lee-Thorp, who faithfully and meticulously edited this book of quiet times. I am grateful to God for your servant spirit and your brilliance.

And thank you, Jack Smith, publisher for Banner Of Truth, for listening to the Lord and making it possible for these books to reach a wider audience.

Thank you, Dottie McDowell, for being my encourager via e-mail and for challenging me to be a woman of faith. Thank you, Josh McDowell, for being my example of a servant of God in ministry. You have been the model to me for Quiet Time Ministries.

A special thank you to the staff and volunteers at Quiet Time Ministries for your hours of tireless service to the Lord. Than you to Kayla Branscum and Myra Murphy for putting together thousands of these books so that others could spend time with the Lord. Thank you to the Dream Team for your faithful support of this ministry. Thank you to Cindy Clark for assisting me and Quiet Time Ministries. You are a very special gift, and I thank the Lord for you.

Thank you, Leann McGee and Elmer Lappen, for discipling me in the importance of a quiet time with God. And a special thanks to Dr. Bill Bright and staff for stressing the great value of spending time with God during my years with Campus Crusade for Christ.

Finally, thank you to all the men and women whose hearts for God have inspired and challenged me, especially A. W. Tozer, Amy Carmichael, Oswald Chambers, F. B. Meyer, Andrew Murray, Mrs. Charles Cowman, Hannah Whitall Smith, J. I. Packer, Ann Kiemel Anderson, Elisabeth Elliot, Jim Elliot, Kay Arthur, Ney Bailey, and Dr. Bill Bright.

BORN A SOUL
NAÏVE BLISS
VICTIM OR VICTOR
EARTHLY VENTURE IS THIS.

Elizabeth Stuter Snyder

Let us throw off everything that hinders and the sin that so easily entangles, and let us run with perseverance the race marked out for us.
Hebrews 12:1

your quiet time with the Lord

As a junior in college I sat in a room listening to a man talk about commitment to Jesus Christ. I was excited to hear his message as I had big dreams of what God could do in and through me in the future. The speaker continued his message and then, all of a sudden, he stopped, leaned forward—gazing into our excited faces—and said, "You know, statistics show that in ten years only a very small percentage of you will be walking closely with the Lord." We were stunned. I guess we could identify in a small way with the twelve disciples when Jesus said one of them would betray Him. We could not believe it. But you know what? Ten years later, few of us were walking closely with the Lord.

I have observed that there are two kinds of Christians: those who know and love the Lord and walk closely with Him, and those who do not. What makes the difference? One primary thing: much time alone with God. There are those who cultivate their relationships with God, and those who do not.

Is knowing God your great desire? And yet, does it seem impossible to find time alone with Him? Perhaps you have never taken some quiet time to sit and talk with God. Such time is an absolute necessity if you desire to know Him. Even Jesus had a quiet time: "Jesus often withdrew to lonely places and prayed" (Luke 5:16).

The most common question people ask is, "Where do I begin in my quiet time?" It is an awesome thing to think about spending time with God, the Creator of the universe, King of kings, and Lord of lords. To establish and maintain a quiet time with the Lord, it will be helpful for you to set aside a time, a place, and a plan.

THE TIME

Choose a time when you may be alone with God and free from distraction. The morning is usually the best, but for some it may be late at night. Ask God for creativity in setting aside this time, especially if you have many responsibilities. It will vary depending upon the stage of your life.

The most important principle in setting aside time is to allow God to determine such elements as the time, length, and location of your quiet time. According to God, time with Him is not optional—it's imperative. It is absolutely vital to growth in your relationship with Him. Keep in mind that quality time leads to quality of relationship. The more time you spend with God, the more intimate your relationship with Him will be. Intimacy with God is the goal.

THE PLACE

Choose a place for your quiet time that is free of distraction. Organize all your quiet time materials in this place. You may wish to use a basket to hold your quiet time materials, or a bookshelf in your office. You may vary the location of your quiet time by going to a quiet restaurant, a park, a mountain retreat, or the beach. The following are helpful materials for your quiet time:

- Cross-reference Bible (New International Version or New American Standard Bible)
- Quiet time notebook or journal (a special notebook is available from Quiet Time Ministries)
- Pen/pencils, cassette recorder/CD player, praise or worship tapes/CDs
- Devotional reading, hymnbook
- Exhaustive concordance, word study tools, different Bible translations such as *The Message*, The New Living Translation, The Amplified Bible, The Williams New Testament

THE PLAN

In your quiet time, God speaks to you in His Word and you speak to Him in prayer. Because the Bible is God's Word, it is authoritative as the manual for your life. Paul encourages you to be extravagant with God's Word by allowing it to "dwell in you richly" (Colossians 3:16).

Your quiet time plan should include different devotional disciplines to draw you into God's Word, hear Him speak, and respond to Him in prayer. There are many disciplines of devotion based on biblical principles that will help you draw near to God. A discipline of devotion is not a negative concept. Henri Nouwen defines *discipline* as "the effort to create some space in which God can act. Discipline means to prevent everything in your life from being filled up. Discipline means that somewhere you're not occupied, and certainly not preoccupied. In the spiritual life, discipline means to create that space in which something can happen that you hadn't planned or counted on."[1]

Disciplines of devotion that help create space in which God can act include writing in a journal, meditating on Scripture or classic devotional books, solitude, devotional Bible study, listening to God, prayer, submission to God, and personal application of biblical truths. Your quiet-time plan serves as a guideline and resource to remind you of all the devotional disciplines. You may not do the same thing every day in your time with God. A plan will challenge you to experiment with new ways of drawing near to God.

How exciting it is that we, as God's children, may spend time with Him. This book of quiet times uses a plan that includes many devotional disciplines to help you draw near to God. It is designed according to the acrostic P.R.A.Y.E.R.™

Prepare your heart
Read and study God's Word
Adore God in prayer
Yield yourself to God
Enjoy His presence
Rest in His love

How to Use This Book

You have in your hands a unique and exciting devotional study. Each quiet time is organized according to the P.R.A.Y.E.R.™ plan just outlined. Each element of this plan offers devotional reading, devotional Bible study, hymns, Scripture for meditation, word studies, suggested journal writing, and prayers related to the specific topic for the day. Journal Pages and Prayer Pages are included in the back of this book. In your quiet times, you will be given opportunities to write in your journal or write a prayer to God. All you need is your Bible and this book for a rich time alone with the Lord.

This book is divided into eight weeks, with five days of quiet times per week. Some quiet times are longer than others. Days 6–7 are given to completing your quiet times and meditating on favorite quotes or Scripture from the week.

Pilgrimage of the Heart is designed to be flexible. You may choose to take more than one day with each quiet time (for example, you may extend the study to sixteen weeks by doing days 1–3 in one week and days 4–7 in the subsequent week). There is so much rich devotional reading and Bible study that you will want to return to favorite readings, Scripture, and prayers again and again.

The blessings are multiplied when you can share what you are learning with others. This devotional book may be used with a group or a friend. Quiet Time Ministries offers a leader's guide with discussion questions for that purpose. You may wish to meet with friends on a weekly or monthly basis to share what God is teaching you. There are also accompanying messages on videotapes and audiotapes for your encouragement or for use in a group study. These quiet-time resources are available from Quiet Time Ministries at *www.quiettime.org* or toll free at 1-800-925-6458, or P.O. Box 14007, Palm Desert, California, 92255.

About the Psalms

I have chosen the Psalms as the subject of this book of quiet times because God has used them in a powerful way to deepen my relationship with Him. James Montgomery Boice believes the Psalms are the deepest and most spiritual portion of the Word of God.[2] Martin Luther loved the Psalms, using them as his daily prayer book as a monk and as the topic of his initial lectures as a professor.[3] When illness and weakness kept him from preaching, Charles Spurgeon found great comfort in the Psalms and, as a result, penned his classic devotional commentary, *The Treasury of David*. This powerful hymnbook of the Hebrew people and early church has found its way into prison cells, lonely hospital rooms, palaces, and deserts. And it is my prayer that it will find its way into your heart and life as well.

The Psalms allow you a glimpse into the quiet times of God's people. They allow you to enter into private conversations between God and those who loved and delighted in Him. Because many of the psalms are prayers to God, you will learn how to pray. Because they are written records, you will learn how to write in your journal. Because they are meditations of Scripture, you will learn how to meditate on God's truth. Because many are the result of silence before God, you will learn how to be still and know that He is God.

PILGRIMAGE OF THE HEART

In the Psalms you see the great pilgrimage of God's servants. It is a pilgrimage of the heart. To be on pilgrimage means *to find your home in God while journeying in a foreign land until you reach your grand destination: heaven.* A great part of your goal in life is to be God's pilgrim. J. I. Packer describes your journey this way: "We are in the position of travelers who, after surveying a great mountain from afar, traveling round it, and observing how it dominates the landscape and determines the features of the surrounding countryside, now approach it directly, with the intention of climbing it."⁴ This is what life is all about. And it takes time.

As you resolve to draw near to God, you will reap the tremendous eternal benefits of time alone with Him. Your life will be transformed in a powerful way. I encourage you to commit time each day to be alone with God, to read His Word, to meditate on the devotional readings, to pray, and to write in your journal using *Pilgrimage of the Heart.*

Are you willing to be God's pilgrim and to launch out on the great journey of contemplating the fathomless, tasting the infinite, and delighting in God's incomprehensible love? If so, gather your materials, set aside a time, find a place, and draw near to your great God.

As you embark on this magnificent pilgrimage of the heart, I would not have you simply watch a travelogue on the Holy Land. I desire that you touch for yourself the blades of grass on the Mount of Olives and watch the sun glisten on the Sea of Galilee. My prayer is that you will "taste and see that the LORD is good" (Psalm 34:8).

LETTER TO GOD

As you begin your adventure with God, take some time now to ask God to bless your time with Him. Where are you in your relationship with the Lord? What have you been learning from Him in the last six months? Write a prayer in the form of a letter to the Lord in the space provided on the next page. Write about those things that have been weighing heavily on your heart. Write out any questions you have about how God works in your life. And don't be afraid to ask God about anything. The Lord says, "Call to me and I will answer you and tell you great and unsearchable things you do not know" (Jeremiah 33:3). Keep His words in mind as you write your letter to Him.

LETTER TO THE LORD

set your heart on pilgrimage

week
one

PSALM 84:1-6

contemplating pilgrimage

How lovely is your dwelling place,
O LORD Almighty!
PSALM 84:1

Prepare Your Heart

Our hearts yearn for that place called home. No matter how many years we spend on earth, or how comfortable we may feel where we live, our hearts long for permanence and security. If you have known God for any length of time, you have discovered that you are, like Abraham, one of the "strangers and exiles on the earth" (Hebrews 11:13, NASB). Your home is with the Lord. He is the place of comfort—your refuge and strength. Thus, you must set your heart on pilgrimage (see Psalm 84:5). What does that mean? This week, in your quiet times with the Lord, you will discover the importance of pilgrimage and how to set your heart on this great journey.

Take some time now to withdraw from earthly things and draw near to the Lord so you can maintain a fixed eye on Him as He leads you. Spend some time in silence, drawing near to God, asking Him to quiet your heart and bless your time together. You may write a brief prayer expressing your thoughts in your Journal in the back of this book. Place all that has been consuming your heart and mind in recent days at the throne of God.

READ AND STUDY GOD'S WORD

Psalm 84 is the focus of your study this week. The author of Psalm 84 is listed in the superscription as one of the "Sons of Korah." Commentators think he was either far away from the temple[1] or, as a Korahite of the third branch of Levi's tribe, assigned the humble work of a doorkeeper at God's temple[2] (see 1 Chronicles 26:1-8). Whether the author was present at the temple or not, he clearly loved being in the temple. That is the point of our study. This psalm is a pilgrimage psalm and describes the believer's desire and faith journey to worship the Lord in His temple. In the Old Testament, the Lord's temple implies the Lord's presence. This psalmist longed to be near God.

1. Read Psalm 84 through once, recording your first impressions.

2. Read Psalm 84 again, meditating on the words. What do you learn about the psalmist's desires, his statements of faith (what he knows to be true about God, God's house, one who is blessed, and so on), and his prayers?

The psalmist's desires

The psalmist's statements of faith (what he knows to be true)

The psalmist's prayers

3. Summarize in two or three sentences your most significant insights about the psalmist's pilgrimage.

4. How would you define *pilgrimage*?

5. How is your pilgrimage like the psalmist's? What can you learn from him that will help you on your journey?

ADORE GOD IN PRAYER

Clement of Alexandria defined prayer as "keeping company with God." Commune with the Lord today using the prayers in Psalm 84. Personalize each prayer. For example, beginning with verse 1 you might say, "How lovely is Your dwelling place, O LORD Almighty. How I long to be near you. You are majestic and holy and worthy of my highest praise." As you talk with the Lord, remember He is the one with whom you will spend all eternity and He is your great Companion on your pilgrimage. Bring any immediate needs and desires to Him. You may wish to write out your prayer requests using the Prayer Pages in the back of this book.

YIELD YOURSELF TO GOD

It is only by leaving home and taking a pilgrimage that we will begin to see how our own stories are interwoven with the great romance God has been telling since before the dawn of time. It is on this pilgrimage that we begin to see that each of us has a part in the cosmic love affair that was created specifically with us in mind. . . . Entering into the sacred romance begins with a decision to become a pilgrim of the heart.[3]

BRENT CURTIS AND JOHN ELDRIDGE IN *THE SACRED ROMANCE*

Do you live as a pilgrim on earth? Have you engaged in the pilgrimage of the heart? You may wish to express your thoughts in your journal at the back of this book.

ENJOY HIS PRESENCE

What was your most significant insight today in your quiet time? Write it out in the space below. Carry that thought with you throughout the day, allowing it to remind you of the Lord's presence in your life.

REST IN HIS LOVE

"And He said, 'My presence shall go with you, and I will give you rest'" (Exodus 33:14, NASB).

the call to pilgrimage

My soul yearns, even faints, for the courts of the LORD;
my heart and my flesh cry out for the living God. . . .
Blessed are those who dwell in your house;
they are ever praising you.

PSALM 84:2,4

Prepare Your Heart

Written across the pages of Scripture in broad strokes is the great invitation of a majestic God of love who invites you, His beloved, to come away with Him. He longs for you to dwell with Him, commune with Him, and delight in Him. He desires to keep company with you every moment of your day. "In [His] presence is fullness of joy; in [His] right hand there are pleasures forever" (Psalm 16:11, NASB).

The greatest thing in all of life is to know God. In Him you will find true meaning and purpose. As you draw near to Him today, listen for His call to your heart: "'For I know the plans I have for you,' declares the LORD, 'plans to prosper you and not to harm you, plans to give you hope and a future. Then you will call upon me and come and pray to me, and I will listen to you. You will seek me and find me when you seek me with all your heart'" (Jeremiah 29:11-13).

O God, the Triune God, I want to want Thee; I long to be filled with longing; I thirst to be made more thirsty still. In Jesus' name. Amen.[1]

A. W. TOZER IN *THE PURSUIT OF GOD*

READ AND STUDY GOD'S WORD

In Psalm 84 we see a great yearning for God. This man knew that God is a *living* God — thinking, feeling, with personality. He wanted to experience God's presence. In those days, men and women could feel the nearness of God most when they were in God's temple. God was present there so that His people could experience and enjoy Him firsthand. God's presence issues forth in His call to pilgrimage. *God's call to pilgrimage is His invitation to His people to find their home in Him.*

1. What do you see in the following verses that invites you to find your home in God? Write your insights and observations as you meditate on each verse.

Deuteronomy 30:1-3,9-10,15-20

Deuteronomy 33:27

Joshua 1:8-9

2 Chronicles 16:9

Psalm 31:19-20

Psalm 71:3

Isaiah 65:1

Jeremiah 31:33-34

John 14:18-23; 15:4

James 4:8

Revelation 21:3

2. Summarize in two or three sentences your most significant insights related to God's invitation to you.

3. Do you long for God? How have you seen this longing in your own life?

4. According to the passages you studied today, how does God respond to your longing for Him?

ADORE GOD IN PRAYER

Write out a prayer to the Lord in your Journal, expressing your desire for Him. Devote one Prayer Page in the back of this book to personal requests related to your relationship with God.

YIELD YOURSELF TO GOD

Why do some persons *find* God in a way that others do not? . . . I venture to suggest that the one vital quality which they had in common was *spiritual receptivity*. Something in them was open to heaven, something which urged them Godward. Without attempting anything like a profound analysis I shall say simply that they had spiritual awareness and that they went on to cultivate it until it became the biggest thing in their lives. They differed from the average person in that when they felt the inward longing they *did something about it*. They acquired the lifelong habit of spiritual response.[2]

A. W. TOZER IN *THE PURSUIT OF GOD*

Will you cultivate spiritual receptivity to God and acquire the lifelong habit of spiritual response?

ENJOY HIS PRESENCE

Take some time now to meditate on what you have learned from the Lord. Think about His invitation to you to dwell with Him. What does His invitation mean to you today? What was your most significant insight that you can carry with you throughout the day?

REST IN HIS LOVE

"Come to Me, all who are weary and heavy-laden, and I will give you rest. Take My yoke upon you and learn from Me, for I am gentle and humble in heart, and you will find rest for your souls. For My yoke is easy and My burden is light" (Matthew 11:28-30, NASB).

the commitment to pilgrimage

Blessed are those whose strength is in you,
who have set their hearts on pilgrimage.
PSALM 84:5

Prepare Your Heart

God's call to pilgrimage is the call to find your home in God and live life here as one who journeys in a foreign land until you reach your grand destination: heaven. Your pilgrimage takes you on an adventure with "the people of God seeking a country."[1]

God's pilgrims "set their hearts on pilgrimage" (Psalm 84:5). This is what I call the "heartset" of a Christian. You've heard of a mindset. A heartset is a deep determination and resolve that flows as a passion from the heart. It is your response to God's call to pilgrimage. It is the determination and resolve to find life where life is really found: in Christ alone.

As you find your dwelling place in God, you realize this world is not your home. There is a better country, a heavenly one. That is what the pilgrimage of the heart is all about. To set your heart on this pilgrimage, you must resolve to develop and cultivate a rich inner life with God. You can do this through prayer, devotional Bible study, silence, solitude, meditating on God's Word, fasting, and submission to God. Set your roots deep down into God and not in the world. Determine to pursue God more than any other single thing.

READ AND STUDY GOD'S WORD

1. Down through the centuries, each man and woman of God has lived a unique pilgrimage on this earth. Read Hebrews 11, the great chapter known as the Hall of Fame of Faith, and record your insights and observations about the pilgrimage of these godly people: "men of whom the world was not worthy" (Hebrews 11:38, NASB). Try reading it in more than one Bible translation as you describe their experiences.

Men of old, or ancients (verses 1-2)

Abel (verse 4)

Enoch (verse 5)

Noah (verse 7)

Abraham (verses 8-12,17-19)

Sarah (verse 11)

All these people (verses 13-16)

Isaac (verse 20)

Jacob (verse 21)

Joseph (verse 22)

Moses' parents (verse 23)

Moses (verses 24-28)

The Israelites (verses 29-30)

Rahab (verse 31)

Gideon, Barak, Samson, Jephthah, David, Samuel, prophets (verses 32-34)

Women (verse 35)

Others, and all these (verse 36-40)

2. How is your pilgrimage similar to the lives of these godly people?

3. Which ones do you identify with the most, and why?

4. What qualities are necessary for your pilgrimage of the heart?

5. Write in your own words what it means for you to set your heart on pilgrimage.

ADORE GOD IN PRAYER

John Bunyan wrote, "Prayer is a sincere, sensible, affectionate, pouring out of the heart or soul to God through Christ, by the strength or assistance of the Spirit."[2] Pour out your heart now to the Lord. Write out Psalm 84:1-5 in your Journal, personalizing it as a prayer to God. Worship the Lord, praising Him for what you have learned about who He is. If there are immediate needs in your life or in your family, write these requests on a Prayer Page and bring them to the Lord.

YIELD YOURSELF TO GOD

> God, I want to give You every minute of this year. I shall try to keep You in mind every moment of my waking hours. I shall try to let my hand write what You direct. I shall try to let You be the speaker and direct every word. I shall try to let You direct my acts. I shall try to learn Your language as it was taught by Jesus and all others through whom You speak—in beauty and singing birds and cool breezes, in radiant Christlike faces, in sacrifices and in tears. It will cost not only much, but everything that conflicts with this resolve.[3]
>
> FRANK LAUBACH IN *MAN OF PRAYER*

Are you more concerned with the things of this world or the things of God (see Matthew 6:33; 1 John 2:15-17)?

Are you cultivating a rich inner life, a spiritual life, learning God's language of prayer and worship?

Do you often draw near to God, your dwelling place? Is your heart open to God (see James 4:8; 2 Chronicles 15:4)?

ENJOY HIS PRESENCE

Begin memorizing Psalm 84:5: "Blessed are those whose strength is in you, who have set their hearts on pilgrimage." What is the result of setting your heart on pilgrimage? The blessing of God. The word *blessing* is used throughout the Bible. The New Testament word for blessing is *makarios*, which means one who possesses God's favor and, as a result of being indwelt by Christ through the Holy Spirit, is fully satisfied no matter the circumstances. "*Makarios* (blessed) is the one who is in the world yet independent of the world; his satisfaction comes from God and not from favorable circumstances."[4] As you think about Psalm 84:5 throughout the day, consider how God is feeding and satisfying you independently of any circumstances.

REST IN HIS LOVE

"This is what the LORD says: 'Stand at the crossroads and look; ask for the ancient paths, ask where the good way is, and walk in it, and you will find rest for your souls'" (Jeremiah 6:16).

the course and character of a pilgrim — part 1

As they pass through the Valley of Baca,
they make it a place of springs;
the autumn rains also cover it with pools.
PSALM 84:6

Prepare Your Heart

You have been thinking about life as a pilgrimage: finding your home in God and living on earth as one who journeys in a foreign land until you reach your destination: heaven. You have seen the necessity of setting your heart on this pilgrimage, resolving to find life in Christ alone, and cultivating a rich inner life with God. What is the landscape of your pilgrimage? What territory can you expect to cover? As you travel, God will develop your character as His child.

The Pilgrim's Progress by John Bunyan, one of the greatest Christian classics of all time, takes the reader on an allegorical adventure with a pilgrim named Christian, who travels from the City of Destruction to the Celestial City of God. On his journey, Christian confronts many obstacles, but by faith he defeats each one as he ultimately holds fast to Jesus Christ. Amazingly, Bunyan wrote this wonderful story while in prison. The greatest works often arise out of extreme adversity.

The territory of the believer changes throughout the course of life. Change is sometimes traumatic and painful. No matter where you are in your life, God's purposes will never be thwarted. Today, as you prepare to draw near to the Lord in His Word and in prayer, take a few moments to think about the question God asked Adam in the Garden of Eden: "Where are you?" What has God been doing in your life and teaching you in the last six months? Write your thoughts in your Journal. Then ask the Lord to speak to you in His Word today.

READ AND STUDY GOD'S WORD

The Scriptures include many different places that characterize the spiritual topography of a believer's life. During the next two days, you will look at some of those places. You will discover that in each place, God develops character qualities in the pilgrim.

The Mountains of Change

You have probably encountered the mountains of change many times. Major life changes test your priorities and affections. Changes also reveal the true nature of your pilgrimage, that you are in a foreign land and your real destination is not money, success, or any other thing, but eternal life with your Lord.

1. Read Psalm 46:1-7. What are some of the changes that can take place in life? Include any additional observations and insights as you read these verses.

2. In this psalm, what is the believer's source of hope and help?

3. What changes has God brought in your life?

4. Where do you turn for hope and help?

The Desert and Wilderness

Have you ever experienced a time in your life when you were afflicted and thirsty, longing for God? A time when you felt totally alone, and God's Word seemed to yield no treasure? Maybe that is your experience even now. In such a time, God will answer you Himself.

5. Read Isaiah 41:17-20. What do you learn about the desert and what God does there?

Observations About the Desert	What God Does

6. In the desert, God develops endurance in the life of the believer. This is "the quality that bears things, not simply with resignation, but with blazing hope because it knows that these things are leading to a goal of glory."[1] Read James 1:2-4. What do you learn about perseverance (endurance)?

7. Summarize what you have learned about the desert experience.

8. If you are in a desert, what truths encourage you?

The Valley of Weeping

On his pilgrimage to the temple, the psalmist of Psalm 84 had to pass through the Valley of Weeping ("Baca"). This valley near Jerusalem may have been called "Baca" or "weeping" because it was lined with tombs.[2] It was a parched, waterless valley where only balsam trees could grow. In the believer's life, this is the dark night of the soul when God seems to withdraw all blessings. You may feel so troubled you cannot speak. The trial may be such that if God does not act, all is lost. In this valley, the foundations of your faith are shaken.

9. Read Psalm 84:6-7. What happens in the Valley of Weeping?

10. What circumstances could bring a person to the Valley of Weeping?

11. In this valley, God builds faith into the believer's life. It is the faith that is able to proclaim, "Though he slay me, yet will I hope in him" (Job 13:15). Read Hebrews 11:1. What do you learn about faith?

12. What have you learned that will help you the next time you are in the Valley of Weeping?

ADORE GOD IN PRAYER

Dietrich Bonhoeffer emphasized the importance of allowing the richness of God's Word—not the poverty of our hearts—to determine our prayers.[3] Today you have taken time to explore the Word of God and have learned many exciting truths about your journey with God. What are some of the most powerful verses you studied? Use these verses as a springboard into worship and adoration of God. Allow God's Word to lead you in prayer about your struggles and adverse circumstances. Does God's Word prompt a prayer about someone in your life?

YIELD YOURSELF TO GOD

In his book *The Green Letters*, Miles J. Stanford shared an illustration that was given by Dr. A. H. Strong. A student asked Strong, the president of his school, "whether he could not take a shorter course than the one prescribed. 'Oh yes,' replied the President, 'but then it depends upon what you want to be. When God wants to make an oak, He takes a hundred years, but when He wants to make a squash, He takes six months.'"[4]

There are no shortcuts to godliness. Your experiences can be the tools God uses to make you the man or woman He wants you to be. Paul said, "We also rejoice in our sufferings, because we know that suffering produces perseverance, perseverance, character; and character, hope. And hope does not disappoint us, because God has poured out his love into our hearts by the Holy Spirit, whom he has given us" (Romans 5:3-5). Are you willing to trust in God as He leads you across the landscape of your pilgrimage, the topography of the soul? If so, hope, endurance, and faith are qualities you can expect to become evident in your life.

Hope is the quality God builds into your character when you face the mountains of change. In his book *Romans, Verse by Verse,* William Newell calls this "Divine Process":

> God brings us into tribulations and that of all sorts; graciously supplying therewith a rejoicing expectation of deliverance in due time; and the knowledge that, as the winds buffeting some great oak on a hillside cause the tree to thrust its roots deeper into the ground, so these tribulations will result in steadfastness, in faith and patient endurance; and our consciousness of steadfastness — of having been brought by grace through the trials,—gives us a sense of Divine approval, or approvedness, we did not before have; and which is only found in those who have been brought through trials, by God's all-sufficient grace. This sense of God's approval arouses within us abounding *hope*—we might also say, *hopefulness,* a hopeful, happy state of soul.

Have you experienced this hope when you encountered a mountain of change?

Endurance is the quality God builds into your character when you are in the desert or wilderness. The Greek word for endurance is *hupomone* and means "to remain under." When this word is associated with trials, it means "to remain under trials and testings in a way that honors God."[5] Have you learned the secret of humbling yourself "under God's mighty hand, that he may lift you up in due time" (1 Peter 5:6)?

Faith is the quality God builds into your life when you are in the Valley of Weeping. It is the spiritual sight God gives you when you take Him at His Word no matter the circumstance or feelings you experience. James McConkey explains that "faith is *dependence* upon God." He explains that dependence on God begins only where dependence on self comes to an end and that sometimes dependence on yourself can only come to an end when "sorrow, suffering, affliction, broken plans and hopes" bring you to a place where you are helpless, defeated, and discouraged. Only then will you discover that you are learning faith in the great classroom of life: "to find your tiny craft of life rushing onward to a blessed victory of life and power and service undreamt of in the days of fleshly strength and self-reliance."[6] In the dark night of the soul, have you learned to immerse yourself in the Word of God, that you might walk by faith and not by sight?

ENJOY HIS PRESENCE

What has influenced your life the most from today's study of the course and character of a pilgrim? As you think about your current circumstances, what have you learned that will make a difference in how you live? If you need more room to write, you may use a page in your Journal.

REST IN HIS LOVE

"After you have suffered for a little while, the God of all grace, who called you to His eternal glory in Christ, will Himself perfect, confirm, strengthen and establish you" (1 Peter 5:10, NASB).

the course and character of a pilgrim — part 2

As they pass through the Valley of Baca,
they make it a place of springs;
the autumn rains also cover it with pools.
PSALM 84:6

Prepare Your Heart

As you continue in your study of the course and character of a pilgrim, ask God to quiet your heart and free your mind from any distractions. Write a prayer in your Journal that expresses your love for God, your desire to be His pilgrim, and your passion to know Him.

READ AND STUDY GOD'S WORD

Today you are continuing your study of the landscape of your pilgrimage. You have seen that this territory includes the mountains of change, the desert or wilderness, and the Valley of Weeping. These are the places where your priorities and affections are tested. God is building into you qualities like hope, endurance, and faith. There is more territory to cover as well. You will find in your travels that you will also experience quiet waters and the high places.

The Quiet Waters and Place of Springs

1. Look at Psalm 84:6. Notice that the place of springs is found in the Valley of Weeping. Have you ever experienced peace and joy in the midst of a painful ordeal? If so, describe your experience.

2. How do you think it's possible for a person to experience the place of springs right in the middle of the Valley of Weeping?

3. Read Psalm 23. Here you find the quiet waters because of the presence of the Lord. What do you learn about the Lord in this psalm?

4. In this place of quiet waters and springs, God gives contentment to you, His pilgrim. What do you learn about contentment from Philippians 4:6-13?

5. What have you learned that will help you experience contentment in the circumstances of life?

The High Places

The high places are the places of pure delight in God Himself. You may enjoy them regardless of your circumstances. For example, the prophet Habakkuk was God's man in a dark and distressing hour. He knew God's judgment on Israel's sins was about to be carried out. God's people would be carried off to exile. Yet Habakkuk was given the glorious experience of the high places.

6. Read Habakkuk 3:16-19. What do you observe about Habakkuk's situation, what he did, and how God responded?

7. In the high places, the Christian pilgrim experiences the gifts of joy, worship, and praise. It has been said that joy is not the absence of suffering but the presence of God. We don't always feel God's presence, but His presence in our lives is always a fact. What was it about God that gave Habakkuk cause to rejoice and worship?

8. Psalm 37:4 says, "Delight yourself in the LORD and he will give you the desires of your heart." What do you think it means to delight in God?

9. How are praise and worship part of the landscape of your pilgrimage?

ADORE GOD IN PRAYER

These last two days you have had the opportunity to explore many exciting passages of Scripture. Praying through Scripture is one of the best ways to learn to pray. Talk with the Lord today about what you have learned in His Word. You might consider choosing to take a prayer walk: Write each significant verse you've read yesterday or today on a three-by-five card. Then go for a walk and pray along the way, using your cards to guide your prayers.

YIELD YOURSELF TO GOD

Yesterday you saw that as you travel across the landscape of your pilgrimage, God transforms you on the inside, making you the person He wants you to be. Contentment and joy are two character qualities He builds in your life as you experience the quiet waters and the high places.

  Contentment is what God produces in you when He leads you to the quiet waters. The Greek word for contentment is *autarkes* and means "the ability to have enough totally independent of external circumstances." It implies sufficiency and competency. In the believer's case, it is sufficiency in Christ. It means to be independent of circumstances because of dependence upon Christ.[1]

Have you learned to be content in every circumstance (see Philippians 4:11)? How can you depend on Christ as the all-sufficient Lord of your life in your present circumstance?

Joy is the quality you will experience when you encounter God's high places. The queen of England has many residences in the United Kingdom. The flag of England is raised at the residence the queen occupies. It has been said that joy is the flag of a Christian that shows the King is in residence. Joy is pure delight in God Himself and is a fruit of the Holy Spirit in your life. Do you ever turn your eyes to God and delight in Him even in the midst of adversity?

ENJOY HIS PRESENCE
Where are you in the course of your pilgrimage? What is God teaching you? Can you see how He is transforming you on the inside? What have you learned that will help you in your pilgrimage? Write your thoughts in your Journal.

REST IN HIS LOVE
"For it is God who is at work in you, both to will and to work for His good pleasure" (Philippians 2:13, NASB).

DEAR FRIEND,

During the next two days, spend some more time with the quiet times on Psalm 84:1-6. You may wish to linger at favorite passages of Scripture, meditate on significant quotes, review prayer requests and record answers to prayer, or write in your Journal. You may wish to consult your commentaries, recording any notes and insights on Psalm 84:1-6. As you think about what you have learned this week, record:

Your most significant insight

Your favorite quote

Your favorite verse

The hope of the pilgrim is centered in the dwelling place of God. The earthly temple suggests the heavenly home. It is a place of rest and of worship. The light of it shines upon the pathway, and is the inspiration of the pilgrimage. The experience of the pilgrim is then described. Faith has an anchorage; it is found in God when the heart is set upon the consummation. Faith has an activity; it passes through dry valleys, and fills them with springs of refreshment. Faith has an assurance; it goes from strength to strength, confident of finally appearing before God. The pilgrim finally pours out his prayer, and it is full of praise and confidence. Its desire is for the vision of God, which by comparison is infinitely to be preferred, even though it be the distant view of a doorkeeper, to all the world has to offer. The lessons of the psalm for all the pilgrims of hope are first, that the heart should be set upon the upper things; secondly that faith may dig wells in driest places and find the living Water; and finally, that pilgrimage develops strength, rather than produces weakness, as these conditions are fulfilled.[1]

G. CAMPBELL MORGAN IN *NOTES ON THE PSALMS*

the journey of the pilgrim

week
two

PSALM 84:7-12

the consistency of the pilgrim

They go from strength to strength. . . .
PSALM 84:7

Prepare Your Heart

The psalmist says that those who set their hearts on pilgrimage "go from strength to strength" (verse 7). This is the pattern of consistency in the believer's life. You will consistently draw upon God's resources, experience spiritual growth, and become a mature pilgrim in Christ.

Thomas Watson said, "Godliness being engraved in the heart by the Holy Ghost, as with the point of a diamond, can never be erased."[1] There is no mistaking the work of God in the heart of a person: "He who began a good work in you will perfect it until the day of Christ Jesus" (Philippians 1:6, NASB).

From outward appearances, your life may appear to be fluctuating with the circumstances of your life. But as a pilgrim of God, you are being renewed day by day. You may be outwardly weak, but when you are weak, He is strong. At times you may be down, but you are not out. You have learned to draw near to God, even in the hard times. As a result, you "go from strength to strength." As you prepare to draw near to the Lord, ask Him to show you His truth from His Word.

READ AND STUDY GOD'S WORD

Today you will think about how you grow spiritually. How does God work in your life? How does His presence make a difference? Don't you find it interesting that He doesn't just save you and then wait until heaven to have a relationship with you?

1. Turn to Jeremiah 31:33-34. What do you learn about the new covenant established by the Lord?

These verses indicate a clear contrast between the law and the new life possible through Jesus Christ. While the new covenant was originally addressed to the people of Israel, this gift of a new and lasting relationship with God is offered to all of us now (see John 1:9-13). A covenant is the most solemn and binding agreement one can make with another. It is the basis of your salvation. God established it through the death and shed blood of His Son, Jesus Christ.

This new covenant is God's promise of the relationship you now enjoy with Him. This type of life with God did not just evolve. God planned it from eternity past. Part of that plan involved Jesus' death on the cross for your sin. When you invite Jesus into your life, ask for forgiveness of your sins, and surrender your life to Him, God establishes a permanent relationship with you. If you have never established a relationship with the Lord, it is imperative that you do so now by praying a simple prayer something like this: "Lord Jesus, I need You. Thank You for dying on the cross for my sins. I ask You now to come into my life, forgive my sins, and make me the person You want me to be. In Jesus' name, Amen."

Once God forgives your sin, He indwells you by His Holy Spirit. You may now know the Lord firsthand, moment by moment. You are His child and His pilgrim, on the way to heaven. As in any relationship, your knowledge of the Lord grows. Because you are now indwelt by the Holy Spirit, something amazing happens. You are changed. Knowing God really does make a difference. Little by little, and sometimes dramatically, you are transformed. This process of spiritual growth is called sanctification.

2. Look at the following verses and record what you learn about how God works in your life. Take time with these verses and you will have a rich experience with the Lord.

2 Corinthians 5:16-17

2 Corinthians 3:17-18

Galatians 2:20

Philippians 1:6; 2:12-13

3. Summarize what you have learned about how God works in your life. How can you "go from strength to strength"?

ADORE GOD IN PRAYER

Today you have learned some powerful truths—truths that you will need eternity to comprehend. Pray today that God will apply these truths to your heart and life. Pray that you will live these truths and grow in the grace and knowledge of Jesus Christ. Also, pray for people in your life to grow in grace and "go from strength to strength."

YIELD YOURSELF TO GOD

Through the years the hungry-hearted believer finds he has been brought a long way, and each step of the way has been personally experienced: reality which springs from faith founded upon the facts of the Word. The more clearly we enter by faith into objective truth, or what is true of us in Christ, the deeper, more experiential, and practical, will be the subjective work in us, and the more complete will be the manifestation of the moral effect in our life and character.[2]

MILES J. STANFORD AND "C. H. M." IN *THE GREEN LETTERS*

Are you walking by faith in God's Word and going "from strength to strength"? Is there any area of your life that you are holding back from the Lord? Will you give this to the Lord and allow Him to transform you, making you a pilgrim who will "grow up in all aspects into Him" (Ephesians 4:15, NASB)?

ENJOY HIS PRESENCE

Think now about what God has done in your life. Take some time to make a memorial to the Lord in your Journal. To do this, take one page and write out the most significant events in your life when God worked in your heart in a powerful way. You might include significant books, people, and times alone with God.

Thank God for how He has worked and how He is working even now. Praise Him for His mighty deeds on your behalf!

REST IN HIS LOVE

"But we all, with unveiled face, beholding as in a mirror the glory of the Lord, are being transformed into the same image from glory to glory, just as from the Lord, the Spirit" (2 Corinthians 3:18, NASB).

the confidence of the pilgrim

. . . till each appears before God in Zion.
PSALM 84:7

Prepare Your Heart

The psalmist says that those on pilgrimage will appear before God in Zion. The pilgrim has the assurance that he or she will reach the desired end. That desired end is heaven and eternal life with God. As you draw near to the Lord in your quiet time, meditate on the words of the beloved hymn "It Is Well With My Soul."

When peace, like a river, attendeth my way,
When sorrows like sea billows roll—
Whatever my lot, Thou hast taught me to say,
It is well, it is well with my soul.

Refrain:
It is well with my soul,
It is well, it is well with my soul.

Tho Satan should buffet, though trials should come,
Let this blest assurance control,
That Christ hath regarded my helpless estate,
And hath shed His own blood for my soul.

My sin   O the bliss of this glorious thought—
My sin, not in part, but the whole,
Is nailed to the cross, and I bear it no more;
Praise the Lord, praise the Lord, O my soul!

And, Lord, haste the day when my faith shall be sight,
The clouds be rolled back as a scroll:
The trump shall resound, and the Lord shall descend,
Even so—it is well with my soul.

HORATIO G. SPAFFORD

READ AND STUDY GOD'S WORD

In your study of pilgrimage, it is imperative that you focus on your hope. That is what gives
you confidence as God's pilgrim. God wants you to be assured of your destiny with Him.
Paul said, "If we have hoped in Christ in this life only, we are of all men most to be pitied"
(1 Corinthians 15:19, NASB). As God's pilgrim on your journey to heaven, what do you look
forward to? That is the subject of your study today. May these truths so stir in your heart that
you will be homesick for heaven.

　1. If you are short on time today, choose four of these passages of Scripture. Take time with
each passage, and ask God to open your eyes so that you might "know the hope to which
he has called you, the riches of his glorious inheritance in the saints" (Ephesians 1:18).

　Matthew 8:11

　Luke 23:39-43

　John 14:1-4

　1 Corinthians 2:9

　2 Corinthians 5:1-10

　2 Corinthians 12:1-4

　Ephesians 1:18

Hebrews 11:16

Hebrews 12:22-24

1 Peter 1:4

2 Peter 1:10-11

2 Peter 3:11-13

Revelation 21:1–22:17

2. Summarize in two or three sentences what you have learned about heaven.

3. In light of your future, how should you live in the present?

4. In what ways do these truths about your future give you confidence in your present life?

ADORE GOD IN PRAYER

You have studied the believer's eternal home and the blessed state of those who are on God's pilgrimage. However, there are those who have not set their hearts on pilgrimage. Their home is this world. Pray today for those in your life who do not know God. You may wish to devote a Prayer Page to those who need to know the Lord. In that way, as you see God working in their lives and answering your prayers, you may record the answer. It is exciting to see God at work. His mission is to seek and save the lost, and we are invited to join in His task. As Jesus said, our food is to do the will of God and accomplish His work (see John 4:34).

YIELD YOURSELF TO GOD

Horatio Spafford, a wealthy businessman, had invested heavily in real estate on the shore of Lake Michigan. As a result of the Chicago Fire of 1871, his land-holdings were wiped out. Just before this disaster, he had lost his only son.

Later, desiring a vacation for his wife and four daughters, he planned to join D. L. Moody on one of his evangelistic campaigns in England. He sent his wife and four daughters ahead of him on the *S. S. Ville du Havre*. On November 22, the ship was struck by another vessel and sank in twelve minutes. Over two hundred lives were lost, including Spafford's four daughters. Spafford received a cable from his wife delivering the news, "Saved alone." Days later, Spafford left by ship to join his wife. It is said that at the exact spot where his daughters drowned, Spafford wrote the words, "When peace, like a river, attendeth my way, / When sorrows like sea billows roll. . . . " Although he had lost what was most dear to him, he was able by grace to say, "It is well with my soul." How is that possible? Read the lines of the fourth stanza again:

> And, Lord, haste the day when my faith shall be sight,
> The clouds be rolled back as a scroll:
> The trump shall resound, and the Lord shall descend,
> Even so — it is well with my soul.

Do you see the hope of heaven? Will you be encouraged today with the hope of a glorious future in heaven?

ENJOY HIS PRESENCE

Take some time now to think about what heaven will be like. In silence and solitude, turn your thoughts to heaven. What were your most significant insights as you spent time with the Lord? Thank the Lord for what He has shown you. Write a prayer to Him in your Journal, expressing what is on your heart.

REST IN HIS LOVE

"See how very much our heavenly Father loves us, for he allows us to be called his children, and we really are!" (1 John 3:1, NLT).

"I am convinced that nothing can ever separate us from his love. Death can't, and life can't. The angels can't, and the demons can't. Our fears for today, our worries about tomorrow, and even the powers of hell can't keep God's love away. Whether we are high above the sky or in the deepest ocean, nothing in all creation will ever be able to separate us from the love of God that is revealed in Christ Jesus our Lord" (Romans 8:38-39, NLT).

the conversation of the pilgrim

Hear my prayer, O LORD God Almighty;
listen to me, O God of Jacob.
PSALM 84:8

Prepare Your Heart

When the psalmist cries out, "Hear my prayer, O LORD God Almighty," we see the conversation of God's pilgrim. It is a special conversation, for it is a conversation with God, the Creator of the universe. The great privilege granted to all God's pilgrims is prayer. Pouring out one's soul to God is the life breath of the believer.

The marvelous truth is that God loves prayer. He loves to hear the cries of His people, and He acts on our behalf when we talk to Him. Will you enter the very throne room of God and kneel at His throne of grace, by faith, that you might "receive mercy and find grace to help [you] in [y]our time of need" (Hebrews 4:16)? Meditate on the words of the following prayer as a preparation for your time with God today.

In Prayer

O LORD,
In prayer I launch far out into the eternal world,
and on that broad ocean my soul triumphs
over all evils on the shores of mortality.
Time, with its gay amusements and cruel disappointments
never appears so inconsiderate as then.
In prayer I see myself as nothing;
I find my heart going after thee with intensity,

and long with vehement thirst to live to thee.
Blessed be the strong gales of the Spirit
that speed me on my way to the New Jerusalem.
In prayer all things here below vanish,
and nothing seems important
but holiness of heart and the salvation of others.
In prayer all my worldly cares, fears, anxieties disappear,
and are of as little significance as a puff of wind.
In prayer my soul inwardly exults with lively thoughts
at what thou art doing for thy church,
and I long that thou shouldest get thyself a great name
from sinners returning to Zion.
In prayer I am lifted above the frowns and flatteries of life,
and taste heavenly joys;
entering into the eternal world
I can give myself to thee with all my heart,
to be thine forever.
In prayer I can place all my concerns in thy hands,
to be entirely at thy disposal,
having no will or interest of my own.
In prayer I can intercede for my friends, ministers,
sinners, the church, thy kingdom to come,
with greatest freedom, ardent hopes,
as a son to his father
as a lover to the beloved.
Help me to be all prayer and never to cease praying.[1]

FROM *THE VALLEY OF VISION: A COLLECTION OF PURITAN PRAYERS AND DEVOTIONS*

What phrase is your favorite from this prayer today, and why?

READ AND STUDY GOD'S WORD

We develop a life of prayer in an intimate, ongoing relationship with the Lord. God has given us many examples in His Word of those who cultivated this life of prayer. Among those examples is Jehoshaphat, who became king of Judah after King Asa died.

1. Read 2 Chronicles 17:1–19:11 and record everything you learn about Jehoshaphat. You may want to mark each occurrence of Jehoshaphat's name (and related pronouns) with a colored pencil.

What is most significant to you about Jehoshaphat and his relationship with the Lord?

2. Read 2 Chronicles 20 and record everything you learn about prayer, including:
   Jehoshaphat and his prayer

   The people's worship of God

   The result of their prayer

3. Summarize what you learn from Jehoshaphat's example about:
   Prayer

   How to respond in difficult situations

4. How would you define *prayer*?

Adore God in Prayer

Has your study in God's Word today prompted prayer in your heart? You may write this prayer in your Journal or simply bring it to the Lord now. Will you be like Jehoshophat and bow with your face to the ground, falling down in worship before the Lord (see 2 Chronicles 20:18)? As you pray, inquiring of the Lord and seeking His help (see 2 Chronicles 20:3-4), you may want to turn to your Prayer Pages and write out a number of requests related to the people and circumstances in your life. Consider these verses on prayer: "Pray about everything" (Philippians 4:6, NLT); "Do not be afraid or discouraged because of this vast army. For the battle is not yours, but God's" (2 Chronicles 20:15); "Always pray and [do] not give up" (Luke 18:1).

Yield Yourself to God

The first and chief need of our Christian life is *fellowship with God*. The Divine life within us comes from God, and is entirely dependent upon Him. As I need every moment afresh the air to breathe, as the sun every moment afresh sends down its light, so it is only in direct, living communication with God that my soul can be strong. . . . Begin each day by tarrying before God, and letting Him touch you. Take time to meet God. To this end, let your first act in your devotion be a setting yourself still before God. In prayer, or worship, everything depends upon God taking the chief place. I must bow quietly before Him in humble faith and adoration, speaking thus within my heart: *God is. God is near. God is love, longing to communicate Himself to me.* God, the Almighty One, Who worketh all in all, is even now waiting to work in me, and make Himself known. Take time, till you know God is very near.[2]

ANDREW MURRAY IN *THE DEEPER CHRISTIAN LIFE*

"O God, you are my God, earnestly I seek you; my soul thirsts for you" (Psalm 63:1). As you read these words, allow them to penetrate your heart, and meditate on the great blessing of drawing near to God. Then, today, will you pray?

ENJOY HIS PRESENCE
Meditate on this verse: "I waited patiently for the LORD; And He inclined to me and heard my cry" (Psalm 40:1, NASB).

REST IN HIS LOVE
"And we can be confident that he will listen to us whenever we ask him for anything in line with his will. And if we know he is listening when we make our requests, we can be sure that he will give us what we ask for" (1 John 5:14-15, NLT).

the comfort of the pilgrim

Better is one day in your courts than a thousand elsewhere;
I would rather be a doorkeeper in the house of my God
than dwell in the tents of the wicked.
PSALM 84:10

Prepare Your Heart

Life displays a profound paradox: the wicked seem to prosper and the godly seem to suffer. However, this psalmist has discovered a truth that the wicked can never know unless they turn from their wicked ways. There is something *better* than anything here on earth: better than riches, better than material things, better than success, better than fame, better than earthly relationships. This better thing is the great comfort to the pilgrim of the Lord, a comfort found in the courts of the Lord. Why? Because the Lord is there, and He is better than any other pursuit in life. He is the source of every good thing for the pilgrim. In Him is mercy, grace, and help in time of need. In fact, He is "the God of all comfort" (2 Corinthians 1:3).

The Christian pilgrim may enjoy the courts of the Lord even now, by faith. How is this possible? By drawing near to God and living in His presence. In our inner life, we may see Him by faith. This faith is not a feeling so much as a certainty based on the facts of His revelation to us. He has revealed Himself to us three ways: in the creation of heaven and earth, in Jesus Christ, and in the Bible. That is why it is so vital to spend time in His Word; there we may know His ways and character that we may know Him (see Exodus 33:13).

God's Word is heard best when you are silent and your soul is quiet. Dietrich Bonhoeffer described the necessity of a silent, still, quiet time with God in His Word: "The Word comes not to the chatterer but to him who holds his tongue. . . . Silence is the simple stillness of the individual under the Word of God. . . . We are silent after hearing the Word because the Word is still speaking and dwelling within us."[1] Spend a few moments in silence, preparing your heart to enter the courts of the Lord, where you will meet alone with your Lord, the God of all comfort.

READ AND STUDY GOD'S WORD

What does the pilgrim experience when drawing near and entering the courts of the Lord? And what comfort is there in a pilgrimage that may include suffering? That is the subject of our study today.

   1. One of the great personalities in the Bible is Paul. Paul was a contemporary of Jesus and His disciples. He was a Pharisee and so zealous for his Jewish faith that he saw the followers of Jesus as an extreme threat. He believed they were working against God, so he set out to destroy the church. Read Acts 8:1-3 and 9:1-31. What do you learn about Paul's character and experiences (also known as Saul)?

   2. Once you meet Jesus Christ and set your heart on pilgrimage, you will never be the same. You will love the courts of the Lord, for there you may enjoy fellowship with Jesus Christ. There is no one like Him. Paul discovered this. In Philippians 3:8 he shared his goal in life. Meditate on the following translations of Philippians 3:8, and record your insights as you observe the different words and phrases the translators have used to convey the Greek words accurately. Think about what God wants you to know from these verses. What do you see in these verses about Paul's goal in life?

    More than that, I count all things to be loss in view of the surpassing value of knowing Christ Jesus my Lord, for whom I have suffered the loss of all things, and count them but rubbish so that I may gain Christ. (NASB)

    Nay, I even reckon all things as pure loss because of the priceless privilege of knowing Christ Jesus my Lord. And for his sake I have suffered the loss of everything, and reckon it all as mere refuse, in order that I may win Christ and be found in union with him. (The New Testament in Modern Speech)[2]

Yes, furthermore I count everything as loss compared to the possession of the priceless privilege (the overwhelming preciousness, the surpassing worth and supreme advantage) of knowing Christ Jesus my Lord and of progressively becoming more deeply and intimately acquainted with Him [of perceiving and recognizing and understanding Him more fully and clearly]. For His sake I have lost everything and consider it all to be mere rubbish (refuse, dregs), in order that I may win (gain) Christ (the Anointed One). (AMP)

3. Paul considered it a fact that Jesus Christ may be experientially known in this life. You may enter the courts of the Lord each day and fellowship with the Lord Jesus and the Father through the Holy Spirit. Jesus said, "If anyone loves Me, he will keep My word; and My Father will love him, and We will come to him and make Our abode with him. . . . The Helper, the Holy Spirit, whom the Father will send in My name, He will teach you all things, and bring to your remembrance all that I said to you" (John 14:23,26, NASB). Look at the following translations of John 14:22-23. Describe the kind of relationship these verses say you can have with the Lord.

Judas (not the Iscariot) asked, "Master, how is it that you will reveal yourself clearly to us and not to the world?" "If anyone loves me," replied Jesus, "he will obey my teaching; and my Father will love him, and we will come to him and make our home with him." (The New Testament in Modern Speech)[3]

Judas, (not Judas Iscariot) said to Him, "Why is it, Lord, that you are going to make yourself real to us and not to the world?" Jesus answered him, "If anyone really loves me, he will observe my teaching, and my Father will love him, and both of us will come in face-to-face fellowship with him; yes, we will make our special dwelling place with him." (WMS)

4. In Jesus Christ you may find great comfort even if suffering is part of your pilgrimage. Look at the following verses and record what you learn about your Lord Jesus Christ:
Matthew 11:28-30

1 Corinthians 1:30

Ephesians 1:3

Hebrews 1:1-4

Hebrews 4:15-16

5. Summarize your most significant insights from these verses about your Lord.

6. In what ways do these truths bring comfort to you?

ADORE GOD IN PRAYER

Spend some time in worship of your Lord. Look at each truth you have learned about Jesus and thank Him for who He is. As you dwell on who He is, bring each burden on your heart to Him.

YIELD YOURSELF TO GOD

As you have received Christ Jesus the Lord, so walk in Him.

COLOSSIANS 2:6 (NASB)

The first act of the Christian life is to receive Christ, and every moment afterward we must continue receiving him. The act must become an attitude. Breathe in the love and power of Jesus. Take deep breaths. Then we shall be rooted in him in secret, and built up in him in our outward walk and behavior. If we have Christ, we have all God's fullness. Like Jacob's ladder, he links us with God. . . . We have everything in Jesus. He has fulfilled the Law in all respects on our behalf. Let us put the waters of entire surrender and consecration between our past, our sins, and the world, and rise into his life, the life of resurrection glory and power.[4]

F. B. Meyer in Devotional Commentary

Enjoy His Presence

My Jesus, I Love Thee

My Jesus, I love Thee, I know Thou art mine;
For Thee all the follies of sin I resign;
My gracious Redeemer, my Savior art Thou:
If ever I loved Thee, my Jesus, 'tis now.

I love Thee because Thou hast first loved me,
And purchased my pardon on Calvary's tree;
I love Thee for wearing the thorns on Thy brow:
If ever I loved Thee, my Jesus, 'tis now.

I'll love Thee in life, I will love Thee in death,
And praise Thee as long as Thou lendest me breath;
And say when the death-dew lies cold on my brow:
If ever I loved Thee, my Jesus, 'tis now.

In mansions of glory and endless delight,
I'll ever adore Thee in heaven so bright;
I'll sing with the glittering crown on my brow:
If ever I loved Thee, my Jesus, 'tis now.

William R. Featherstone

Rest in His Love

"Blessed be the God and Father of our Lord Jesus Christ, the merciful Father and the all-comforting God, who comforts me in every sorrow I have, so that I can comfort people who are in sorrow with the comfort with which I am comforted by God. For just as my sufferings for Christ are running over the cup, so through Christ my comfort is running over too" (2 Corinthians 1:3-5, WMS).

the claims of the pilgrim

For the LORD God is a sun and shield;
the LORD bestows favor and honor;
no good thing does he withhold
from those whose walk is blameless.
O Lord Almighty,
blessed is the man who trusts in you.
PSALM 84:11-12

Prepare Your Heart

Whenever a study of a passage of Scripture comes to a close, you may feel sad because you don't want to leave this beautiful place. It is the same feeling you experience when you get on the plane to go home after enjoying a fascinating city. Florence, Italy, houses sculptures by Michelangelo, museums with some of the finest Renaissance art, and the simple beauty of red-tiled roofs nestled like jewels in the Tuscan mountains, with church bells ringing in the background. Psalm 84 is like the Florence, Italy, of Scripture. There is so much treasure in one small chapter of the Bible. This demonstrates the profound nature of God's Word. As you prepare to draw near to the Lord today, meditate on the words of this pilgrimage prayer.

Journeying On

Lord of the cloud and fire,
I am a stranger, with a stranger's indifference;
My hands hold a pilgrim's staff,
My march is Zionward,
My eyes are toward the coming of the Lord,

My heart is in thy hands without reserve.
Thou hast created it,
redeemed it,
renewed it,
captured it,
conquered it.
Keep from it every opposing foe,
crush in it every rebel lust,
mortify every treacherous passion,
annihilate every earthborn desire.
All faculties of my being vibrate to thy touch;
I love thee with soul, mind, body, strength,
might, spirit, affection, will,
desire, intellect, understanding.
Thou are the very perfection of all perfections;
All intellect is derived from thee;
My scanty rivulets flow from thy unfathomable fountain.
Compared with thee the sun is darkness,
all beauty deformity,
all wisdom folly,
the best goodness faulty.
Thou art worthy of an adoration greater than my dull heart can yield;
Invigorate my love that it may rise worthily to thee,
tightly entwine itself round thee,
be allured by thee.
Then shall my walk be endless praise.[1]

FROM *THE VALLEY OF VISION: A COLLECTION OF PURITAN PRAYERS AND DEVOTIONS*

READ AND STUDY GOD'S WORD

God's pilgrims on God's pilgrimage will confront obstacles. These obstacles may come in many forms: illness, loss of a job, financial ruin, oppression, depression, disappointment, death of a dream, a broken relationship, a difficult marriage, a difficult child, incarceration of a family member, substance abuse by a loved one, or death of a loved one. What is your response when faced with obstacles? What will help you during these times in your life? The promises of God. These promises are the claims of a pilgrim. They are the pilgrim's rock and shelter, enabling the believer to stand firm regardless of the winds that blow through his or her life. The claims of God's pilgrim anchor your soul to God.

    1. Meditate on Psalm 84:11-12. What are the promises found in these verses?

Which promise means the most to you today?

2. Turn to Exodus 14. Through Moses, God had just led the people of Israel (over six hundred thousand of them) out of Egypt. Everything looked good until something happened. Then the people appeared doomed for disaster. What do you learn from Exodus 14 about God's promise and how He fulfills it?

Exodus 14:17-18 illustrates that when you encounter an obstacle, God accomplishes at least two things: He causes others to know Him and He is glorified. In this event, the people responded in fear. However, because Moses knew and believed God's promise, he was not afraid and he responded with great confidence in God. As a result of this obstacle, the people of Israel became more intimate with God and gained a new respect for His chosen leader, Moses (see Exodus 14:31).

3. Look at the following verses and record what you learn about God's promises:
Isaiah 55:10-11

Matthew 5:18

Matthew 7:24-25

2 Corinthians 1:20

4. *Optional*: What are some of God's promises? If you have extra time today, look at the following verses and record what God has promised. Remember that these are your claims, the claims of God's pilgrim. If you are pressed for time, you may choose one verse today and then return to this section on days 6–7.
Matthew 6:25-34

John 3:16

John 15:7

Romans 8:28-39

Philippians 4:6-7

Philippians 4:19

1 John 2:25; 5:11-12

1 John 3:2

5. How can you apply what you have learned to your own situation? What obstacle do you face? As you think about Psalm 84:11-12 and the other claims of a pilgrim, what promises do you need to claim today?

ADORE GOD IN PRAYER

Exodus 15:1-18 is one of the great prayers in the Bible, sung by Moses and the people of Israel after God delivered them out of the hands of Pharaoh and the Egyptians. Using this prayer as a guide, personalize it into your own prayer to the Lord. You may choose to write your personalized prayer in your Journal.

YIELD YOURSELF TO GOD

"O LORD Almighty, blessed is the man who trusts in you." By his disciplined response to nostalgia the psalmist has found the blessing of those "who have not seen and yet believed" (John 20:29), and can teach us to treat our present state of glimpses and longings as he treated his: not only as a spur to pilgrimage but as a chance to respond to God already in delighted trust.[2]

DEREK KIDNER IN *TYNDALE OLD TESTAMENT COMMENTARIES: PSALMS 73–150*

Have you learned the blessed discipline of delighted trust in God?

ENJOY HIS PRESENCE

Think about the importance of God's promises in your life today. How do they help you as God's pilgrim? As you face the circumstances of your own life, find a portion of God's Word that encourages you and stand strong in that promise.

REST IN HIS LOVE

"O taste and see that the LORD is good; how blessed is the man who takes refuge in Him! O fear the LORD, you His saints; for to those who fear Him, there is no want. The young lions do lack and suffer hunger; but they who seek the LORD shall not be in want of any good thing" (Psalm 34:8-10, NASB).

Dear Friend,

For the next two days, you may desire to spend more time with what you have studied during the week. Meditate on favorite quotations and passages of Scripture. Record in your Journal your most significant insight on pilgrimage from your time in Psalm 84. Write a prayer to the Lord in your Journal, expressing all that is on your heart. As you think about what you have learned this week, record:

Your most significant insight

Your favorite quote

Your favorite verse

Turn your thoughts to the combination: "the Lord God is a sun and a shield." As a sun he shows me more and more of my sinfulness; but then as a shield, he gives me power to oppose it and assurance that I shall conquer. . . . As a sun, he makes me daily more and more sensible of the utter impossibility of my working out a righteousness of my own; but then as a shield, he fastens constantly my thoughts on that righteousness of his Son, which is meritoriously conveyed to all who believe on his name. As a sun, in short, he brings facts to my knowledge, which would make the matter of deliverance seem out of reach and hopeless if he were not at the same time a shield; but seeing that he is both, a shield as well as a sun, the disclosures which he makes as a sun only prepare me for the blessing he imparts as a shield. . . . As a sun, God shows me myself; as a shield, God shows me himself. The sun discloses mine own nothingness; the shield, Divine sufficiency.[1]

CHARLES SPURGEON IN *THE TREASURY OF DAVID*

the song of the pilgrim

week three

PSALM 13

when it seems like forever

How long, O LORD? Will you forget me forever?
PSALM 13:1

Prepare Your Heart

Do you ever feel like everything and everyone is against you? Do you ever feel like no matter how hard you try, the events of your life become more turbulent? David, one of God's choice servants, felt like that. The prophet Samuel anointed David king of Israel when David was only a shepherd boy (see 1 Samuel 16). Did he become king right away? No! In fact, for years it seemed he would be killed or exiled before any of God's promises could be fulfilled.

First, his father sent him back out to shepherd the sheep while his brothers followed King Saul to war. Then David's father sent him to carry provisions to his brothers on the front lines. There David observed Goliath's taunts against God and His people. With great courage, David fought and killed Goliath. This remarkable victory brought David accolades from the people of Israel and respect from Saul's army. That praise angered Saul, and "from that time on Saul kept a jealous eye on David" (1 Samuel 18:9).

Twice Saul tried to kill David with his spear. Saul was afraid of him because the Lord granted him great success in whatever he did (see 1 Samuel 18:14-15). Even Saul's two children, Jonathan and Michal, loved David. When Saul realized this, "he remained his enemy the rest of his days" (1 Samuel 18:29). David had to flee for his life. Hiding in fields, deserts, and caves, he was pursued by Saul. At every turn, Saul narrowly missed finding and killing him. Eventually, David fled to the land of Israel's enemies, the Philistines. Along with six hundred followers, he settled in Ziklag, the southernmost border in the Western Negev, for a year and four months. David finally realized that Saul would eventually destroy him.

Here was a man who had God's promise to be king. With his life constantly in danger and always on the run, far away from all he knew and loved, his trial became prolonged. Possibly he even felt abandoned by God. This was the probable context for Psalm 13, the subject of our study this week. We know by the content of this psalm that David's trial was long and his life was in danger. He repeated "How long" four times in Psalm 13.

Have you ever felt like David? Forgotten by God, in a trial that seems to stretch out far beyond what you ever imagined? You are now experiencing what David experienced: the silence of God. Can there be a song in this desolate land of anguish and sorrow? That is the subject of your quiet times this week. Draw near to God now and ask Him to speak to you today.

READ AND STUDY GOD'S WORD

1. Psalm 13 was written by David, the man after God's own heart. Keeping in mind the context previously described, read Psalm 13. Record any significant insights and observations. What is your first impression of this psalm?

2. Notice that this psalm is a prayer. Read Psalm 13 again and record the main contents of David's prayer.

3. As David began this psalm, what were his main feelings? What do you think he was experiencing when he wrote this psalm?

4. To understand the most likely context for this psalm, read 1 Samuel 27:1-12. David had already been on the run for a long time, hiding in caves, hills, and the desert. Years earlier, the prophet Samuel had anointed David as the next king of Israel. What do you learn from this passage about the events that contributed to David's writing of Psalm 13? (If you desire to read the entire background of events, read 1 Samuel 16–27.)

David's trial was so prolonged that he felt God had forgotten him. Here was a man who loved God, who knew God's character, and who followed after Him wholeheartedly. Yet he felt forgotten by the One he loved most. He expressed those feelings to God.

F. B. Meyer described the background of this psalm: "Saul's persecutions probably lasted for eight or nine years; and no hope of termination appeared (1 Samuel 27:1). David was as a man who spends five hundred days passing through a forest: the tangled over-growth hides the sun; and he begins to despair of ever emerging. Some say this psalm is the cry of the Church (Rev. 6:10)."[1]

Alan Redpath describes David's situation: "In this depressed mood David was saying, in effect, 'I am afraid the Lord has undertaken something more than He can accomplish. I know that He has kept me so far, but the situation is getting too tough for Him; sooner or later Saul is going to get hold of me. After all, it is stupid to attempt the impossible. I have waited for the Lord long enough, and I'm tired of waiting. It is time I took things into my own hands and used my own wits to get out of this situation.'"[2]

Have you ever felt like that? The trial has seemed to go on forever. The cry of your heart echoes David's words, "How long, O LORD?" And you wonder if God has abandoned you or forgotten you. The Bible speaks to this issue.

5. Look up the following verses and record what you learn about God. Keep in mind the immediate context of each passage of Scripture.

Genesis 7:23–8:1 (The Hebrew word for *remember* does not mean to simply recall to mind or to refresh one's memory. It means to express concern and to visit one with gracious love. God "remembered Noah" just when all seemed hopeless. He "paid special attention to Noah and lavished His loving care on him."[3])

Isaiah 49:14-16

Lamentations 3:22-26

6. What can you know is true when a trial seems prolonged and you feel forgotten by God?

ADORE GOD IN PRAYER

The Deeps

LORD JESUS,
Give me a deeper repentance,
a horror of sin,
a dread of its approach;
Help me chastely to flee it,
and jealously to resolve that my heart shall be thine alone.
Give me a deeper trust,
that I may lose myself to find myself in thee,
the ground of my rest,
the spring of my being.
Give me a deeper knowledge of thyself
as savior, master, lord, and king.
Give me deeper power in private prayer,
more sweetness in thy Word,
more steadfast grip on its truth.
Give me deeper holiness in speech, thought, action,
and let me not seek moral virtue apart from thee.
Plough deep in me, great Lord, heavenly husbandman,
that my being may be a tilled field,
the roots of grace spreading far and wide,
until thou alone art seen in me,
thy beauty golden like summer harvest,
thy fruitfulness as autumn plenty.
I have no master but thee,
no law but thy will,
no delight but thyself,
no wealth but that thou givest,
no good but that thou blessest,
no peace but that thou bestowest.
I am nothing but that thou makest me,
I have nothing but that I receive from thee,
I can be nothing but that grace adorns me.
Quarry me deep, dear Lord,
and then fill me to overflowing with living water.[4]

FROM *THE VALLEY OF VISION: A COLLECTION OF PURITAN PRAYERS AND DEVOTIONS*

YIELD YOURSELF TO GOD

Listen to an old and beautiful story of how one Christian dreamed that she saw three others at prayer. As they knelt the Master drew near to them.

As He approached the first of the three, He bent over her in tenderness and grace, with smiles full of radiant love and spoke to her in accents of purest, sweetest music.

Leaving her, He came to the next but only placed His Hand upon her bowed head, and gave her one look of loving approval.

The third woman He passed almost abruptly without stopping for a word or glance. The woman in her dream said to herself, "How greatly He must love the first one, to the second He gave His approval, but none of the special demonstrations of love He gave the first; and the third must have grieved Him deeply, for He gave her no word at all and not even a passing look. I wonder what she has done, and why He made so much difference between them?" As she tried to account for the action of her Lord, He Himself stood by her and said: "O woman! How wrongly hast thou interpreted Me. The first kneeling woman needs all the weight of My tenderness and care to keep her feet in My narrow way. She needs My love, thought and help every moment of the day. Without it she would fail and fall.

"The second has stronger faith and deeper love, and I can trust her to trust Me however things may go and whatever people do.

"The third, whom I seemed not to notice, and even to neglect, has faith and love of the finest quality, and her I am training by quick and drastic processes for the highest and holiest service. She knows Me so intimately, and trusts Me so utterly, that she is independent of words or looks or any outward intimation of My approval. She is not dismayed nor discouraged by any circumstances through which I arrange that she shall pass; she trusts Me when sense and reason and every finer instinct of the natural heart would rebel; — because she knows that I am working in her for eternity, and that what I do, though she knows not the explanation now, she shall understand hereafter.

"I am silent in My love because I love beyond the power of words to express, or of human hearts to understand, and also for your sakes that you may learn to love and trust Me in Spirit-taught, spontaneous response to My love, without the spur of anything outward to call it forth."[5]

MRS. CHARLES COWMAN IN *STREAMS IN THE DESERT*

How do you respond to the silences of God? What have you learned today that helps you in your trials? Record your thoughts in your Journal.

ENJOY HIS PRESENCE

What have you learned today that will encourage you when God is silent? What promises from God's Word will sustain you as you wait on Him? Write out one or two verses from God's

Word on three-by-five cards and carry them with you for meditation throughout the day.

> It will be a wonderful moment for some of us when we stand before God and find that the prayers we clamored for in early days and imagined were never answered, have been answered in the most amazing way, and that God's silence has been the sign of the answer.[6]
>
> OSWALD CHAMBERS IN *PRAYER: A HOLY OCCUPATION*

REST IN HIS LOVE

"Can a mother forget the baby at her breast and have no compassion on the child she has borne? Though she may forget, I will not forget you! See, I have engraved you on the palms of my hands; your walls are ever before me" (Isaiah 49:15-16).

when God hides His face

How long will you hide your face from me?
PSALM 13:1

Prepare Your Heart

Meditate on the words of Jeanne Marie De La Motte-Guyon (1648–1717) as you draw near to God today.

> A little bird I am,
> Shut from the fields of air;
> And in my cage I sit and sing
> To Him who placed me there;
> Well pleased a prisoner to be,
> Because, my God, it pleases Thee.
> Naught have I else to do;
> I sing the whole day long;
> And He whom most I love to please
> Doth listen to my song;
> He caught and bound my wandering wing,
> But still He bends to hear me sing.
> Thou hast an ear to hear,
> A heart to love and bless;
> And though my notes were e'er so rude,
> Thou wouldst not hear the less;
> Because Thou knowest, as they fall,
> That love, sweet love, inspires them all.
> My cage confines me round;

Abroad I cannot fly;
But though my wing is closely bound,
My heart's at liberty.
My prison walls cannot control
The flight, the freedom, of the soul.
O, it is good to soar
These bolts and bars above,
To Him whose purpose I adore,
Whose providence I love;
And in Thy mighty will to find
The joy, the freedom, of the mind.

READ AND STUDY GOD'S WORD

In 1944, Hitler's police force, the Gestapo, raided a home in the town of Haarlem in the Netherlands. Corrie ten Boom, her father, and her sister, Betsie, were arrested and jailed. Corrie and Betsie were taken to Ravensbruck, the dreaded women's death camp. Conditions there included long hours of forced labor, rat-infested cold barracks, malnutrition, disease, and physical abuse. It seemed as though God had hidden His face from two of His servants, Corrie and Betsie ten Boom.

However, there is a song God gives even in the night. Corrie and Betsie shared the love of God with hundreds of women in that death camp, many of whom were executed hours later. At night they would huddle together and read the Bible, praying for their release. Corrie learned, during that horrible nightmare, that God is a faithful and loving God.

When God seems to hide His face, the pilgrim learns the great value of drawing near and waiting on Him. David felt as though God had hidden His face when he said, "How long will you hide your face from me?" (Psalm 13:1). Have you ever felt like that? You are not alone. Even Jesus went through this experience. Look at the following events in Jesus' life.

1. Read Mark 15:1-39. How did Jesus deal with a situation in His own life when it appeared that God had hidden His face?

2. Look up the following verses to evaluate God's eternal perspective of these events in Jesus' earthly life:
   Hebrews 5:7-10

Hebrews 9:11-12

Isaiah 53:3-5

3. Summarize your insights in two or three sentences. Think about God's purpose in the suffering Jesus endured when He felt like God was hiding His face.

4. When God seems to hide His face, does it mean He is not with you? The Greek world in the first century believed their gods could have no direct contact with this world or any created being.[1] However, this is not so with our God, the Creator of the heavens and the earth. Meditate on the following verses and record what you learn about God:

Psalm 138:7-8

Psalm 139:1-18

Isaiah 41:10

Isaiah 46:9-11

Isaiah 55:6-13

Jeremiah 23:23-24

5. What can you know is true when it seems as though God is hiding His face?

ADORE GOD IN PRAYER

Perhaps you are feeling the way David did: as though God has been hiding His face in your current circumstances. Stand strong. He is a God who is near. And even if you "dwell in the remotest part of the sea," you can say with the psalmist, "even there Your hand will lead me, and Your right hand will lay hold of me" (Psalm 139:9-21, NASB).

Turn again to Psalm 139:1-18. Choose favorite words and phrases from this passage and, using it as a guide, write a prayer to God in your Journal, personalizing it. For example: "Lord, you have searched me and have known me. You know everything about me. You know where I was this morning. You are with me when I work. You are with me when I drive on the freeway. You are with me when I am sick. . . . "

YIELD YOURSELF TO GOD

> His silence is the sign that He is bringing you into a marvelous understanding of Himself. If God has given you a silence, praise Him, He is bringing you into the great run of His purposes. The manifestation of the answer in time is a matter of God's sovereignty. Time is nothing to God.[2]
>
> OSWALD CHAMBERS IN *PRAYER: A HOLY OCCUPATION*

In what situations is God asking you to wait today? Are you willing to wait on God as He brings about His purposes in your life?

ENJOY HIS PRESENCE

Corrie ten Boom describes a time during roll call at the concentration camp when a cruel guard made the prisoners stand for a long time. Suddenly, a skylark began singing, and all the prisoners turned their eyes heavenward to listen to the song. Corrie thought, "O love of God, how deep and great; far deeper than man's deepest hate." She said that God sent that skylark for three weeks to remind all of them to turn their eyes away from man's cruel hate to the ocean of God's love. One of the great truths Corrie often shared was, "With Jesus the worst can happen, the best remains, and His light is stronger than the deepest darkness."[3] How has God reminded you of His love this week? Look for ways today that God is sending you His love. Meditate on the work of Jesus Christ on the cross: a solid demonstration of the fact that God loves you.

Rest in His Love

"And hope does not disappoint us, because God has poured out his love into our hearts by the Holy Spirit, whom he has given us. You see, at just at the right time, when we were still powerless, Christ died for the ungodly. Very rarely will anyone die for a righteous man, though for a good man someone might possibly dare to die. But God demonstrates his own love for us in this: While we were still sinners, Christ died for us" (Romans 5:5-8).

when i am losing the battle

How long must I wrestle with my thoughts
and every day have sorrow in my heart?
How long will my enemy triumph over me?
PSALM 13:2

Prepare Your Heart

John Bunyan penned the classic allegory *The Pilgrim's Progress* during his imprisonment in the 1600s for preaching the gospel of Jesus Christ. In his story, Christian travels from the City of Destruction to the Celestial City. Along the way he encounters many obstacles and enemies who would deter him from reaching his goal. Some of the most insidious obstacles are found in the Valley of Humiliation and Death. There Christian meets Apollyon, the great enemy of God's people.

Apollyon begins to accuse Christian and, in his rage, hurls fiery darts at him. Christian uses his shield, but as the onslaught of darts increases, he weakens with fatigue, and eventually Apollyon causes him to fall. Apollyon's hideous roaring and threats are such that Christian despairs of life. Crying out, "Rejoice not against me, O mine enemy! When I fall, I shall arise," Christian gives a thrust of his two-edged sword. With that, Apollyon spreads his wings and flies away.

There is a time in a prolonged trial when the pilgrim fears the battle is lost. Surrounded by enemies from without and within, such a pilgrim is weakened and vulnerable. Have you ever found yourself in such a trial? Today you will have the opportunity to learn about your resources in the heat of the battle. Meditate on the words of "I Sing Th' Almighty Power of God" by Isaac Watts (1674–1748) as you draw near to God.

I sing th' almighty power of God,
That made the mountains rise,

That spread the flowing seas abroad,
And built the lofty skies.

I sing the wisdom that ordained
The sun to rule the day;
The moon shines full at His command,
And all the stars obey.

I sing the goodness of the Lord,
That filled the earth with food;
He formed the creatures with His word,
And then pronounced them good.

Lord! How Thy wonders are displayed
Where'er I turn mine eye!
If I survey the ground I tread,
Or gaze upon the sky!

There's not a plant or flower below
But makes Thy glories known;
And clouds arise, and tempests blow,
By order from Thy throne.

Creatures that borrow life from Thee
Are subject to Thy care;
There's not a place where we can flee
But God is present there.

READ AND STUDY GOD'S WORD

Saul has been chasing David for eight years. David is now living in enemy territory in order
to survive. In his weakened condition, feeling abandoned by God, David perceives that his
enemies are conquering him. He faces enemies within as he wrestles with his thoughts and
without as he dodges both Saul and the Philistines.

1. As you begin this study today, review what you learned about David's situation on days
1 and 2. Write in two or three sentences the background of Psalm 13.

2. Read Psalm 13:2. What was troubling David?

3. Is there a circumstance in your life that is causing you to wrestle with your thoughts or experience sorrow in your heart? In what way is your enemy triumphing over you?

4. The Bible is your map for life with a heart set on pilgrimage. In this manual for life, God tells you that you have an enemy who "prowls around . . . seeking someone to devour" (1 Peter 5:8, NASB). Erwin Lutzer describes Satan, your enemy, as the one who wants to make sin look good, sabotage your delight in God, and short-circuit the life God intends for you: a life of power, victory, joy, and peace.[1] Jesus did battle with this enemy and won the victory. Read Matthew 3:16–4:11. List everything you learn about the Enemy's tactics and what Jesus did in the heat of battle.

The Enemy's Tactics	Jesus' Response

5. The best description of Christian spiritual warfare is found in Ephesians 6:10-18. Read this passage and list everything you learn that will help you in spiritual warfare. Be certain to observe what you learn about your enemy.

6. When enemies surround you, it is important to know God's perspective. What can you know about your God when you are in the heat of the battle? Record your insights as you explore the following verses in Scripture:

Joshua 23:8-11

2 Chronicles 20:17-18

Jeremiah 20:11

1 John 4:4

7. Finally, what can you know is the ultimate fate of your enemy according to Revelation 20:7-10?

8. What have you learned that will help you in times when you feel you are losing the battle and are surrounded by enemies?

Adore God in Prayer

Turn to Ephesians 6:13-17 and, in prayer to God, put on each piece of God's armor: the belt of truth around your waist, the breastplate of righteousness, the gospel of peace for your feet, the shield of faith, the helmet of salvation, and the sword of the Spirit—the Word of God.

YIELD YOURSELF TO GOD

In what ways is Satan, the Enemy of your soul, trying to defeat you today? Do you recognize that God is greater than your enemy? Will you claim God's victory over your sin and walk in newness of life today? Will you ask Him to fill you with His Holy Spirit so that you may be controlled and empowered by God (see Ephesians 5:18)? Do you recognize that the Lord is your champion and that He will fight your battles? Draw near to Him right now and thank Him for His power and strength in your life.

ENJOY HIS PRESENCE

The strength of an earthly general lies in his troops—he flies upon their wings. If their feathers get clipped or their necks broken, he is helpless. But in the army of saints, the strength of the whole host lies in the Lord of hosts. God can overcome His enemies without help from anyone, but His saints cannot so much as defend the smallest outpost without His strong arm. One of God's names is "the Strength of Israel" (1 Samuel 15:29). He was the strength of David's heart. With Him, this shepherd boy could defy the giant who defied a whole army; without God's strength, David trembled at a word or two that dropped from the Philistine's mouth. He wrote, "Blessed be the Lord my strength, which teacheth my hands to war, and my fingers to fight" (Psalm 144:1). The Lord is likewise your strength in your war against sin and Satan.[2]

WILLIAM GURNALL IN *THE CHRISTIAN IN COMPLETE ARMOUR*

REST IN HIS LOVE

"Do you not know? Have you not heard? The LORD is the everlasting God, the Creator of the ends of the earth. He will not grow tired or weary, and his understanding no one can fathom. He gives strength to the weary and increases the power of the weak. Even youths grow tired and weary, and young men stumble and fall; but those who hope in the LORD will renew their strength. They will soar on wings like eagles; they will run and not grow weary, they will walk and not be faint" (Isaiah 40:28-31).

when God is my only hope

Look on me and answer,
O LORD my God. Give light to my eyes, or I will sleep in death;
my enemy will say, "I have overcome him,"
and my foes will rejoice when I fall.
PSALM 13:3-4

Prepare Your Heart

Somewhere in the darkness is the imperceptible glimmer of hope that comes to the heart of a pilgrim during a trial. The recognition of hope may be the result of a friend's prayer, intercession by Jesus your Lord, who always lives to intercede for you (see Hebrews 7:25), or the Holy Spirit, who intercedes with "groans that words cannot express" (Romans 8:26). This grain of hope leads the pilgrim to cry out to "the One and Only" (John 1:14). It turns the pilgrim's eye from poverty of soul to the greatness and sufficiency of God. Today, as you meditate on God's Word, turn your eyes to the possibilities that exist in God's answer. Consider and give way to hope in God.

READ AND STUDY GOD'S WORD

1. King Asa of Judah found himself in a desperate situation, surrounded by fierce enemies. Greatly outnumbered, he had no hope of a victory. Read 2 Chronicles 14. What did Asa do? How did God respond? Record your insights and observations.

ADORE GOD IN PRAYER

Turn to Asa's prayer in 2 Chronicles 14:11. Write it out word for word in your Journal and personalize it to fit your own situation. Draw near to the Lord and meditate on each phrase of this prayer, allowing the words to become the cry of your heart.

YIELD YOURSELF TO GOD

Where in your life have you lost hope? Will you, today, open your heart to the God of deliverances and impossibilities? Will you believe Him for those things only He can do? Spend a few moments laying every impossible situation in your life at the feet of the One who is greater than any circumstance or enemy you face today.

ENJOY HIS PRESENCE

> I believe the Lord allows many things to happen on purpose to make us feel our need of Him. The more you find Him in your sorrows or wants, the more you will be attached to Him and drawn away from this place where the sorrows are, to Him in the place where He is. "Set your affection on things above" (Col. 3:2a).[1]
>
> J. B. STONEY IN *THE GREEN LETTERS* BY MILES J. STANFORD

REST IN HIS LOVE

"So do not fear, for I am with you; do not be dismayed, for I am your God. I will strengthen you and help you; I will uphold you with my righteous right hand" (Isaiah 41:10).

when i can finally sing

But I trust in your unfailing love;
my heart rejoices in your salvation.
I will sing to the LORD,
for he has been good to me.
PSALM 13:5-6

Prepare Your Heart

The winds can rage, the sky can be dark, and yet a bird can sit in the hollow of a tree and sing the most beautiful song. The bird is created to sing and God has given it the song. The bird does not sing because of the storm but in spite of the storm. In the same way, there is a point in the trial where finally you are able to turn from despair to trust in the love of God. At long last, you see truths that stand firm, no matter the darkness. Those truths give you a reason to rejoice. They become the words of the song that God gives you in the dark night of the soul. And then, you can finally sing.

Fanny Crosby (1820–1915), one of the greatest hymn writers our world has known, was blind from six weeks of age. Yet she wrote more than eight thousand hymns in her lifetime. She said that her blindness was no mistake. "I verily believe it was His intention that I should live my days in physical darkness, so as to be better prepared to sing His praises and incite others so to do. I could not have written thousands of hymns—many of which, if you will pardon me for repeating it, are sung all over the world—if I had been hindered by the distractions of seeing all the interesting and beautiful objects that would have been presented to my notice."[1]

At the age of eight, Fanny wrote the following words:

O what a happy soul am I!
Although I cannot see,

I am resolved that in this world
Contented I will be.
How many blessings I enjoy,
That other people don't.
To weep and sigh because I'm blind,
I cannot and I won't.[2]

She even remarked that if she were given the choice, she would choose blindness because when she got to heaven the first face she would ever see would be the face of Christ, her Savior. Fanny Crosby studied and memorized Scripture. That was the foundation of her strong faith. Her mother and grandmother made certain she knew the Bible better than any other book. God gave her not just one song but over eight thousand songs! And she shared them with the world.

As you begin your quiet time today, meditate on one of her most well-known hymns, "Blessed Assurance."

Blessed assurance, Jesus is mine!
O what a foretaste of glory divine!
Heir of salvation, purchase of God,
Born of His Spirit, washed in His blood.

Refrain:
This is my story, this is my song,
Praising my Savior all the day long;
This is my story, this is my song,
Praising my Savior all the day long.

Perfect submission, perfect delight!
Visions of rapture now burst on my sight;
Angels descending brings from above
Echoes of mercy, whispers of love.

Perfect submission—all is at rest,
I in my Savior am happy and blest;
Watching and waiting, looking above,
Filled with His goodness, lost in His love.

READ AND STUDY GOD'S WORD

1. It is interesting to note what David did just before he was able to sing. Read Psalm 13 again, and observe his change in perspective from the beginning of the psalm to the end.

As you observe what happened just before he was able to sing, what do you think changed David's perspective?

2. God is the One who gives the song in the night. The following passages all refer to songs by God's people. What do you learn about their songs, and what kinds of things do the singers sing about?

Exodus 15:1-3

Psalm 28:7

Psalm 33:1-5

Psalm 40:1-3

Psalm 77:6-15

Psalm 96:1-6

Psalm 98:1

Psalm 118:13-16

Acts 16:22-28

Ephesians 5:19-20

Colossians 3:16

Revelation 14:1-5

Revelation 15:1-4

3. Summarize in two or three sentences what you have learned about the song God gives.

ADORE GOD IN PRAYER

For your time of prayer, listen to some of the songs from one of your favorite praise/worship recordings. As you listen, turn the gaze of your heart to the Lord and thank Him for all that He has done for you. Thank Him for everything that you know to be true from the Word of God.

YIELD YOURSELF TO GOD

In the book *Songs for Renewal* by Janet Lindeblad with Richard Foster, the authors speak of the relationship between music and our life of devotion with God. They point out that it is the heart that links the two. Music gives wings to the words of prayer in the heart. As the old proverb says, "The one who sings prays twice."[3] Sometimes music says from the heart what a word can never crystallize.

It is very necessary to be brought to the stage of trust in our experience of suffering; perhaps we are brought to it most acutely when we have to look up mutely to God and say "I don't understand it at all, but go on with what you are doing." That marks a real stage of learning to trust in God, and it is a step towards something still further on. Spiritual experience has begun; suffering has already deepened the soul.[4]

OSWALD CHAMBERS IN CHRISTIAN DISCIPLINE

I know it is not the sense of His presence, it is the fact of His presence that is our strength and stay. And yet it is comforting when a mother makes some little sign or speaks some little word to a child who does not see her. And when our Father deals so tenderly with us, then we are very humbly grateful and we store such memories in our heart. And when there is not any feeling we rest on His bare word, "Lo, I am with you always, all the days, and all day long," and are content. The bright flowers of the edelweiss waiting to be gathered among the rough rocks of difficult circumstances—we may call the consolations of God what we will—who are we that we should find such comforts anywhere? Love prepared, Love planted, Love led us to these enchanting discoveries. A child cannot bear to enjoy a delight alone, it turns to its nearest friend with a shout of joy and shares its treasures. Turn so to thy Nearest, soul beloved, speak thy quick thanks and share thy joy. Forget not the Giver in the gift.[5]

AMY CARMICHAEL IN GOLD BY MOONLIGHT

Samuel Rutherford once said, "It is possible to gather gold, where it may be had, with moonlight." This gold, I believe, often comes in the form of a song in the night, to one who, after the long trial, is finally able to sing. Have you ever been given a song in the midst of a dark circumstance? What was the comfort God gave you? Was it a verse from the Bible, an encouragement from a friend, or perhaps an event that seemed to turn the tide of despair in your heart to joy? How has God enabled you to sing in the midst of your daily circumstances?

ENJOY HIS PRESENCE

What have you learned today about the song from the Lord? Has God given you a new song to sing to Him? If you were to write a song to the Lord, what would be the theme? Write your thoughts in your Journal.

REST IN HIS LOVE

"I will give you the treasures of darkness, riches stored in secret places, so that you may know that I am the LORD, the God of Israel, who summons you by name" (Isaiah 45:3).

DEAR FRIEND,

Take these next two days to think about what you have learned from Psalm 13 and the life of David. You may choose to spend more time in some of the verses or with some of your favorite devotional writing and record any additional insights and observations in your Journal. You may wish to consult your commentaries and any other study materials related to Psalm 13. As you think about what you learned this week, record:

Your most significant insight

Your favorite quote

Your favorite verse

The fact that we feel abandoned itself means that we really know God is there. To be abandoned you need somebody to be abandoned by. Because we are Christians and have been taught by God in Scripture, we know that God still loves us and will be faithful to us, regardless of our feelings. So what do we do? We pray, as David does. . . . David's prayer has three requests: "Look on me"; "Answer"; and "Give light to my eyes." If you are suffering from a sense of feeling abandoned by God, which is what this psalm is about, I cannot tell you when the emotional oppression will lift. But it will lift. The curtain of your despair will rise, and behind the veil you will see the blessed Lord Jesus Christ, who has been with you and has loved you all the time.[1]

JAMES MONTGOMERY BOICE IN *PSALMS*

the refuge of the pilgrim

week
four

PSALM 46

have you found your refuge?

God is our refuge and strength,
an ever-present help in trouble.
PSALM 46:1

Prepare Your Heart

During World War II, Hitler's army hunted down, captured, and killed Jews. This was a time of great terror for the Jews and for anyone who helped them. The ten Boom family took a strong stand and decided to help the Jews, protecting them from danger and arranging for their safe passage out of Holland. To do this, the ten Booms had a secret room built in their house. Many Jewish people came to their home for safety and were hidden in this little room. It was a hiding place for the Jews, protecting them from being captured and killed.

In your daily struggles, you need a place of protection, somewhere that is safe for you to hide. This week you are going to discover that God has provided a hiding place for you, no matter what you are facing. Your goal is to learn about your place of refuge and how to run for cover there in the storms of life.

As you begin this week of quiet times with the Lord, take time to draw near to the Lord and lay your burdens at His feet. Ask Him to open your eyes and speak to your heart.

READ AND STUDY GOD'S WORD

The Scripture passage for your study this week is Psalm 46, written by the sons of Korah. These men were the temple choir David had appointed to serve in the temple liturgy. There are twelve psalms written by the sons of Korah: Psalms 42, 44–49, 84–85, and 87–88.

Psalm 46 comes alive when you know its historical context. Imagine you are the king of God's people. God's enemy, the king of Assyria, is attacking you. The Assyrian army comes to the very walls of your city and shouts thunderous threats that you and your people are going to be destroyed. To make matters worse, you then receive a letter from your enemies, outlining exactly how they are going to destroy you. They tell you that your God is completely power-less to help you. What will you do? This was the situation for Hezekiah, the king of God's people. He knew how to make the Lord his refuge. Hezekiah found God to be stronger and more powerful than the circumstance that threatened to destroy him.

1. Turn to 2 Kings 18–19 and read the life event that is thought by most commentators to be the historical context of Psalm 46. How did Hezekiah take refuge in the Lord?

2. The sons of Korah wrote Psalm 46 as a celebration of this victory of God's deliverance. This celebration records great truths about your refuge. Read Psalm 46 and write down your insights related to the following:

What you learn about God

What you learn about life circumstances

What your response is to be

3. In this psalm the pilgrim of God learns that there is a refuge: God Himself! What kind of refuge is your God? Turn to the following verses and record your insights and observations:

Deuteronomy 33:26-29

2 Samuel 22:1-20,33-51

Psalm 73:21-28

Psalm 91

ADORE GOD IN PRAYER

In what way do you need the Lord as your refuge, strength, and help today? Turn to your refuge now and pour out your heart to Him. What is burdening your heart that you can lay at His feet? Record on one of your Prayer Pages each area where you need God as your refuge. Then tell the Lord what you learned about Him that gives you cause for joy today. You may want to write a prayer to the Lord expressing all that is on your heart.

YIELD YOURSELF TO GOD

All other refuges are refuges of lies, all other strength is weakness, for power belongs to God: but as God is all-sufficient, our defense and might are equal to all emergencies. . . .

He never withdraws himself from his afflicted. He is their help, truly, effectually, constantly; he is present or near them, close at their side and ready to give relief, and this is emphasized by the word "very". He is more present than friend or relative can be, yes, more nearly present than even the trouble itself. To all this comfortable truth is added the consideration that his assistance comes at the needed time. He is not as the swallows that leave us in the winter; he is a friend in need and a friend indeed. When it is very dark with us, let brave spirits say, "Come let us sing the forty-sixth Psalm:

> A fortress firm, and steadfast rock,
> Is God in time and danger;
> A shield and work in every shock,
> From foe well-known or stranger."[1]

CHARLES SPURGEON IN THE TREASURY OF DAVID

ENJOY HIS PRESENCE

As you think about what you learned today, consider the following: Why does the Christian need a refuge? What is it about God as our refuge that answers all our deepest needs? What is your most significant insight about God as your refuge that you will carry with you today?

REST IN HIS LOVE

"For in the day of trouble He will conceal me in His tabernacle; in the secret place of His tent He will hide me; He will lift me up on a rock" (Psalm 27:5, NASB).

where is God in the storm?

There is a river whose streams make glad the city of God,
the holy place where the Most High dwells.
God is within her, she will not fall;
God will help her at break of day.
PSALM 46:4-5

Prepare Your Heart

What a question we have before us today. One of the great preachers of all time, Charles Spurgeon, often felt the impact of this great question: "Where is God in the storm?" There was no one who knew biblical truth in his day more than Spurgeon. No one could preach like he could. Yet Spurgeon suffered from tremendous bouts of depression. Perhaps you are a Christian worker, a pastor, a president of a corporation, a father with tremendous responsibilities, or a mother of small children. No matter what your sphere of service, most likely you are expected to have it all together and to be responsible, positive, and successful. These same expectations weighed heavily on the heart of the "prince of preachers," Charles Spurgeon.

What puts our hand once again to the plow so that we can move on in the path God has set before us? It is the discovery of God in the midst of the storm. As you draw near to the Lord today, read Psalm 46 again, prayerfully, in the stillness of the presence of God.

READ AND STUDY GOD'S WORD

One of the greatest lies the Enemy of our souls ever tries to tell the world and us is that God is distant, that He is not interested, and in fact, at times abandons us. When those words shout loudly outside your city walls, you need to know what is true. You need to hear it from God Himself. God does not lie. You can count on what He says. If He says it, that settles it.

Then it is up to you to decide what you are going to believe is true: His Word, or thoughts and feelings that are in conflict with what God says.

The psalmist tells us in Psalm 46:4-5 that even when the earth is giving way and the mountains are falling into the sea, "there is a river whose streams make glad the city of God, the holy place where the Most High dwells. God is within her, she will not fall; God will help her at break of day." When *everything* is falling apart, God is still there, in your midst. He has not moved. And His presence makes a difference.

Look at the following verses and record your insights about the Father, Jesus Christ, and the Holy Spirit. Note specifically who God is, where He is, and what He does.

Psalm 139:1-3

Matthew 28:18-20

John 14:15-21

John 16:12-15

Ephesians 3:20

Philippians 4:19

2 Corinthians 3:4-5

Hebrews 13:5-6

Romans 8:10-18

ADORE GOD IN PRAYER

Turn to your Prayer Pages and outline areas where you need God as your refuge. Pray through each area today and claim the promises you discovered in God's Word. Talk with the Lord about how thankful you are for the most significant truths you learned about Him today. Enjoy His presence in a place of solitude during your time of prayer.

YIELD YOURSELF TO GOD

Hannah Whitall Smith shares in her classic book *The God of All Comfort*:

The thing that helped me personally more than anything else to come to a conviction that God was really enough for me was an experience I had some years ago. It was at a time in my religious life when I was passing through a great deal of questioning and perplexity, and I felt that no Christian had ever had such peculiar difficulties as mine before. There happened to be staying near me just then for a few weeks a lady who was considered to be a deeply spiritual Christian, and to whom I had been advised to apply for spiritual help. I summoned up my courage, therefore, one afternoon and went to see her, pouring out my troubles; I expected of course that she would take a deep interest in me, and would be at great pains to do all she could to help me.

She listened patiently enough, and did not interrupt me; but when I had finished my story, and had paused, expecting sympathy and consideration, she simply said, "Yes, all you say may be very true, but then, in spite of it all, there is God." I waited a few minutes for something more, but nothing came, and my friend and teacher had the air of having said all that was necessary.

"But," I continued, "surely you did not understand how very serious and perplexing my difficulties are."

"Oh, yes, I did," replied my friend, "but then, as I tell you, there is God." And I could not induce her to make any other answer. It seemed to me most disappointing and unsatisfactory. I felt that my peculiar and really harrowing experiences could not be met by anything so simple as merely the statement, "Yes, but there is God." I knew God was there, of course, but I felt I needed something more than just God; and I came to the conclusion that my friend, for all her great reputation as a spiritual teacher, was at any rate not able to grapple with a peculiar case such as mine.

However, my need was so great that I did not give up with my first trial, but went to her again and again, always with the hope that she would sometime begin to understand the importance of my difficulties and would give me adequate help. It was of no avail. I was never able to draw forth any other answer. . . . And, at last, because she said it so often and seemed so sure, I began to dimly wonder whether after all God might not be enough, even for my need, overwhelming and peculiar as I felt it to be. From wondering I came gradually to believing that, being my Creator and Redeemer, He must be enough; and at last a conviction burst upon me that He really was enough, and my eyes were opened to the fact of the absolute and utter all-sufficiency of God.

My troubles disappeared like magic, and I did nothing but wonder how I could ever have been such an idiot as to be troubled by them, when all the while there was God, the Almighty and all-seeing God, the God who had created me, and was therefore on my side, and eager to care for me and help me. I had found out that God was enough, and my soul was at rest.

Have you learned that God is with you and that He is enough? What does that truth mean to you in your life today? Record your insights in your Journal.

ENJOY HIS PRESENCE

What have you learned about God and His presence in your life that you will carry with you today? What is your most significant insight from your time with the Lord?

REST IN HIS LOVE

"The LORD replied, 'My Presence will go with you, and I will give you rest'" (Exodus 33:14).

who is with you in the storm?

The LORD Almighty is with us.
PSALM 46:7

Prepare Your Heart

It is one thing to know that you have a refuge. However, it is quite another to know and understand the nature of your refuge. The psalmist who has written this great psalm celebrates two particular names of God in reference to the great victory over the Assyrians. Today you will learn about the first name: the Lord Almighty.

Why are the names of God so important? Any name of God is a new revelation of His being and character. In Proverbs we learn, "The name of the LORD is a strong tower; the righteous run to it and are safe" (Proverbs 18:10). Today, as you begin your quiet time, draw near to God and ask Him to teach you about who He is, so that you might learn to run to Him and find safety.

READ AND STUDY GOD'S WORD

The name Lord Almighty is Lord Sabaoth in the Hebrew and means "Lord of hosts." These hosts may include the armies of Israel as well as of heaven. When God reveals Himself through this name, He conveys the greatness of His mighty power and His absolute sovereignty over all other powers in the universe, including earthly powers. If you have no hope of deliverance in your situation, then you need to understand that He is the Lord Almighty. If you have no one to help you, no strength of your own, and no earthly resource, then you may run to your Lord-Sabaoth, the Lord of hosts.

1. One of the greatest examples of someone taking refuge in the Lord Almighty is
   David facing Goliath. Read 1 Samuel 17:32-51 and record your insights related to the
   following:

David's challenge

David's attitude

David's action

The results

Summarize what you learned about the Lord Almighty, including His character and ways.

2. Turn to the following verses and write down what you learn about the Lord Almighty:
   2 Samuel 5:9-10

   Psalm 89:5-18

Isaiah 6:1-8

Jeremiah 10:6-7

Jeremiah 31:35

Jeremiah 32:26-27

3. Summarize in two or three sentences what you have learned about God as you have studied His name, the Lord Almighty.

ADORE GOD IN PRAYER
Turn to Psalm 145 and pray this powerful psalm to the Lord. Imagine that you are in God's presence (and you are) and that these are the things you desire to express to God from your own heart.

YIELD YOURSELF TO GOD
In his book *Knowing God*, J. I. Packer compares the life of the early church with that of the twentieth-century church:

> We are unlike the Christians of New Testament times. Our approach to life is conventional and static; theirs was not. The thought of "safety first" was not a drag on their enterprise as it is on ours. By being exuberant, unconventional and uninhibited in living by the gospel they turned their world upside down, but you could not accuse us

twentieth-century Christians of anything like that. . . . We feel that the risks of out-and-out discipleship are too great for us to take. In other words, we are not persuaded of the adequacy of God to provide for all the needs of those who launch out whole-heartedly on the deep sea of unconventional living in obedience to the call of Christ.[1]

In seasons of severe trial, the Christian has nothing on earth that he can trust, and is therefore compelled to cast himself on his God alone. When his vessel is on its beam-ends, and no human deliverance can avail, he must simply and entirely entrust himself to the providence and care of God. Happy storm that wrecks a man on such a rock as this! O blessed hurricane that drives the soul to God and God alone! There is no getting at our God sometimes because of the multitude of our friends; but when a man is so poor, so friendless, so helpless that he has nowhere else to turn, he flies into his Father's arms, and is blessedly clasped therein! When he is burdened with troubles so pressing and so peculiar, that he cannot tell them to any but his God, he may be thankful for them; for he will learn more of his Lord then than at any time. Oh tempest-tossed believer, it is a happy trouble that drives thee to thy Father! Now that thou hast only thy God to trust, see that thou puttest thy full confidence in Him. Dishonour not thy Lord and Master by unworthy doubts and fears; but be strong in faith, giving glory to God. Show the world that thy God is worth ten thousand worlds to thee. Show rich men how rich thou art in thy poverty when the Lord God is thy helper. Show the strong man how strong thou art in thy weakness when underneath thee are the everlasting arms. Now is the time for feats of faith and valiant exploits. Be strong and very courageous, and the Lord thy God shall certainly, as surely as He built the heavens and the earth, glorify Himself in thy weak-ness, and magnify his might in the midst of thy distress.[2]

CHARLES HADDON SPURGEON IN *MORNING AND EVENING*

As you think about who God is as the Lord Almighty, and then reflect on the words of J. I. Packer and Charles Spurgeon, write your thoughts in your Journal. What "Goliaths" are in your life, challenging your faith and the power of God? How does knowing God is the Lord Almighty make a difference in your trust in God?

ENJOY HIS PRESENCE
Today, as you enjoy the presence of Lord Almighty, turn to Psalm 46. Choose one verse in this psalm, memorize it, and carry it with you throughout the day, thinking about all you are learning about the Lord, your refuge.

REST IN HIS LOVE
"Those who know your name will trust in you, for you, LORD, have never forsaken those who seek you" (Psalm 9:10).

who is your fortress?

The God of Jacob is our fortress.
PSALM 46:7

Prepare Your Heart

Martin Luther was born in 1483 in Eisleben, Germany. His education set him on the road to becoming a lawyer. During his training, he came very close to being struck by lightning. This brush with death caused him to decide to become a monk instead. He joined the Augustinian friars and eventually became a professor of theology at the new university at Wittenberg.[1]

Luther loved theology and the study of God's Word. However, the teachings in the book of Romans frustrated him. One day God opened his eyes to the real truth of the gospel. For the first time, Luther saw that in God's righteousness there is not condemnation, but rather justification and salvation, and that it is not by man's works but by faith in Christ alone.

This was a powerful and unique theological change for Luther's day. His teaching of it caused the most powerful men of the day, both civil and religious authorities, to come against him. How did Luther handle the opposition that he faced daily and hourly? He learned to find refuge in God. In fact, Psalm 46 was his favorite psalm. He wrote a hymn based on this psalm, and whenever he became discouraged and depressed during the most difficult times, he would turn to his friend Philipp Melanchthon and say "Come Philipp, let's sing the forty-sixth psalm." Then they would sing the words of that most famous hymn written by Luther: "A Mighty Fortress Is Our God."[2] Today, as a preparation for your time with God, sing this great hymn and meditate on the words.

A Mighty Fortress Is Our God

A mighty fortress is our God,
A bulwark never failing;
Our helper He amid the flood
Of mortal ills prevailing.
For still our ancient foe
Doth seek to work us woe—
His craft and pow'r are great,
And, armed with cruel hate,
On earth is not His equal.

Did we in our own strength confide,
Our striving would be losing,
Were not the right man on our side,
The man of God's own choosing.
Dost ask who that may be?
Christ Jesus, it is He—
Lord Sabaoth His name,
From age to age the same,
And He must win the battle.

And though this world, with devils filled,
Should threaten to undo us,
We will not fear, for God hath willed
His truth to triumph through us.
The prince of darkness grim,
We tremble not for him—
His rage we can endure,
For lo! his doom is sure:
One little word shall fell him.

That word above all earthly pow'rs,
No thanks to them, abideth;
The Spirit and the gifts are ours
Through Him who with us sideth.
Let goods and kindreds go,
This mortal life also—
The body they may kill;
God's truth abideth still:
His kingdom is forever.

MARTIN LUTHER (1483–1546)

READ AND STUDY GOD'S WORD

The second name of God given by the psalmist to celebrate a great victory over Israel's enemies is "the God of Jacob." Understanding Jacob's character and his relationship with God is very important to your understanding of the need to run to God as your refuge. Today your time in God's Word will be devoted to learning about Jacob. Read Genesis 25:19-34 and Genesis 27:1–33:20 as though you were reading a biography. When you have completed this account of many of the important events of Jacob's life, record your insights about the following:

1. What did you see about Jacob's character?

2. What do you think were the most important events in Jacob's life?

3. What do you notice about how God worked in Jacob's life?

4. How was God a refuge for Jacob?

5. What was your most significant insight from the life of Jacob?

ADORE GOD IN PRAYER

Today in your time of prayer, take a few moments to be silent before God. Then thank Him that He is not just Jacob's God but yours also. Talk to Him about what is on your heart today. Turn to Psalm 46 and pray through the words of this psalm, personalizing them as you pray. You may write out your prayer, word for word, in your Journal.

YIELD YOURSELF TO GOD

From our vantage point in history, we know that despite his faulty character Jacob was to become a man of faith and trustworthiness. We see, as he could not, God's design for his life. The tragedy is that he lived so long by his own cunning and cleverness, by a rational self-management that excluded God. For years he lived in the strength of the flesh, directed only by fleshly considerations. Patiently, God let him learn all the hard lessons which accrue to self-centered independence. Jacob acted as though without his self-effort God might make some serious mistakes in his life. Throughout two decades Jacob lived as a manipulator of others; he repeatedly missed God's best and was frustrated continually in a web of his own spinning. Yet God ultimately brought him to a place of dependency and submission, creating through him a people for Himself.[3]

DWIGHT HERVEY SMALL IN *NO RIVAL LOVE*

In what way is God dealing with the Jacob in you? Will you allow God to defeat the self-will and independence so that you can become utterly surrendered and dependent on Him? Only in your weakness can you be strong in the power and might of God. As you think about Jacob and what God is doing in your life, write your thoughts in your Journal. You may include a prayer of submission and surrender to God.

Those who navigate little streams and shallow creeks, know but little of the God of tempests; but those who "do business in great waters", these see His "wonders in the deep." Among the huge Atlantic-waves of bereavement, poverty, temptation, and reproach, we learn the power of Yahweh, because we feel the littleness of man. Thank God, then, if you have been led by a rough road; it is this which has given you your experience of God's greatness and lovingkindness. Your troubles have enriched you with a wealth of knowledge to be gained by no other means: your trials have been the cleft of the rock in which Yahweh has set you, as He did His servant Moses, that you might behold His glory as it passed by. Praise God that you have not been left to the darkness and ignorance which continued prosperity might have involved, but that in the great fight of affliction, you have been capacitated for the outshinings of His glory in His wonderful dealings with you.[4]

CHARLES SPURGEON IN *MORNING AND EVENING*

ENJOY HIS PRESENCE

Look again at Luther's hymn, "A Mighty Fortress Is Our God." Choose one of the stanzas and memorize it, making it your own. Review it often throughout today to turn your thoughts to the God of Jacob, who is also your God.

REST IN HIS LOVE

"[The Lord] said to me, 'My grace is sufficient for you, for my power is made perfect in weakness.' Therefore I will boast all the more gladly about my weaknesses, so that Christ's power may rest on me. That is why, for Christ's sake, I delight in weaknesses, in insults, in hardships, in persecutions, in difficulties. For when I am weak, then I am strong" (2 Corinthians 12:9-10).

what are you to do?

Be still, and know that I am God.
PSALM 46:10

Prepare Your Heart

It is one thing to know that you have a refuge and to know how great that refuge is. However, it is quite another thing to actually run to God as your refuge. How do you do it? The psalmist has said in Psalm 73:28, "I have made the Sovereign LORD my refuge; I will tell of all your deeds." The secret to making the Lord your refuge is found in Psalm 46. The application of these truths will be your goal for today. To prepare your heart, meditate on this Puritan prayer:

Refuge

O LORD,
Whose power is infinite and wisdom infallible,
Order things that they may neither hinder, nor discourage me,
nor prove obstacles to the progress of thy cause;
Stand between me and all strife, that no evil befall,
no sin corrupt my gifts, zeal, attainments;
May I follow duty and not any foolish device of my own;
Permit me not to labour at work which thou wilt not bless,
that I may serve thee without disgrace or debt;
Let me dwell in thy most secret place under thy shadow,
where is safe impenetrable protection from
the arrow that flieth by day,

the pestilence that walketh in darkness,
the strife of tongues,
the malice of ill-will,
the hurt of unkind talk,
the snares of company,
the perils of youth,
the temptations of middle life,
the mournings of old age,
the fear of death.
I am entirely dependent upon thee for support, counsel, consolation.
Uphold me by thy free Spirit,
and may I not think it enough to be preserved from falling,
but may I always go forward,
always abounding in the work thou givest me to do.
Strengthen me by thy Spirit in my inner self
for every purpose of my Christian life.
All my jewels I give to the shadow of the safety that is in thee—
my name anew in Christ,
my body, soul, talents, character,
my success, wife (husband), children, friends, work,
my present, my future, my end.
Take them, they are thine, and I am thine, now and forever.[1]

FROM *THE VALLEY OF VISION: A COLLECTION OF PURITAN PRAYERS AND DEVOTIONS*

READ AND STUDY GOD'S WORD

This week you have learned many powerful truths about God as your refuge. Now, in the storms of life, what will you do? How will you run to Him as your refuge? That is what you will think about today.

1. Turn to Psalm 46 and read it again, this time looking for everything the psalmist is to do. Record your insights here.

The most profound action that a pilgrim is to take on his or her pilgrimage is "Be still, and know that I am God." "Be still" means Stop! Surrender! Lay down your weapons! Cease from all your own efforts! Then rest in God, His character, and His ways. Does this verse mean that we are to be passive in this life? No! At times we are very active, "always abounding in the work of the Lord, knowing that [our] toil is not in vain in the Lord" (1 Corinthians 15:58, NASB). What then, does this mean in practical application? You are going to look at one example in the Old Testament: Jonah. God asked Jonah to do something. But Jonah wanted to do something else, so he ran from God. Jonah needed to *be still and know* that God was God.

2. Read Jonah 1–4 and record your insights about the following:

The character and ways of Jonah

The character and ways of God

Jonah's attitude toward God and His ways

How Jonah eventually heeded the words, "Be still, and know that I am God."

The result

3. *Optional:* Look at the following verses and record what you learn about stillness and God's character:

    1 Chronicles 29:11-14

    Isaiah 30:15

    Isaiah 32:17

    Hosea 2:14

    Micah 6:8

    Zephaniah 3:17

4. What qualities do you think are necessary in your life to enable you to be still and know that He is God?

5. How does God encourage this stillness in your life?

6. What does it mean to surrender to God? How do you do it?

ADORE GOD IN PRAYER

Turn to your Prayer Pages and list areas of your life where you need to run to God as your refuge. Take these requests to the Lord, and as you talk with God, include biblical truths you have learned from your study this week. You may need to look back through your study to refresh your memory of all that you have learned. It is important to pray not only from the depth of your own need, but also from the wealth of God's truth in His Word.

YIELD YOURSELF TO GOD

Give God time to reveal Himself to you. Give yourself time to be silent and quiet before Him, waiting to receive, through the Spirit, the assurance of His presence with you, His power working in you. Take time to read His Word as in His presence, that from it you may know what He asks of you and what He promises you. Let the Word create around you, create within you a holy atmosphere, a holy heavenly light, in which your soul will be refreshed and strengthened for the work of daily life.

Andrew Murray applied these words in his life after a painful experience. He spent a long time with the Lord, then wrote,

First, He brought me here, it is by His will I am in this strait (narrow, tight) place: in that fact I will rest. Next, He will keep me here in His love, and give me grace to behave as His child. Then, He will make the trial a blessing, teaching me the lessons He intends me to learn, and working in me the grace He means to bestow. Last, in His good time He can bring me out again—how and when He knows. Let me say I am here (1) by God's appointment, (2) in His keeping, (3) under His training, (4) for His time.[2]

ANDREW MURRAY IN *THEY FOUND THE SECRET*

In what way, in your present circumstances, do you need to be still and know that He is God? Write your thoughts in your Journal. As you think about this, write three or four truths that you can count on from what you have learned in Psalm 46.

ENJOY HIS PRESENCE

What were your most significant insights about how to be still and know that He is God? What did you learn about God today that encourages you to surrender yourself and your circumstances to Him?

REST IN HIS LOVE

"So be content with who you are, and don't put on airs. God's strong hand is on you; he'll promote you at the right time. Live carefree before God; he is most careful with you. . . . So keep a firm grip on the faith. The suffering won't last forever. It won't be long before this generous God who has great plans for us in Christ—eternal and glorious plans they are!— will have you put together and on your feet for good. He gets the last word; yes, he does" (1 Peter 5:6-7,9-11, MSG).

DEAR FRIEND,

What a week of study it has been in one of the great psalms of the Bible! Take the next two days to review what you learned each day. You may want to spend more time in some of your favorite passages from your study this week. Then turn to the comments of others on Psalm 46 in commentaries and study Bibles. Close with a prayer of thanksgiving, praising God for who He is as your great refuge. As you think about what you have learned this week, record:

Your most significant insight

Your favorite quote

Your favorite verse

Comment on this great song of confidence seems almost unnecessary, so powerfully has it taken hold upon the heart of humanity, and so perfectly does it set forth the experience of trusting souls in all ages, in circumstances of tempest shock. The system of the song is worth noting. It is divided into three parts. The first (verses 1-3) is the challenge of confidence. The second (verses 4-7) tells the secret of confidence. The third (verses 8-11) declares the vindication of confidence.

The challenge announces confidence in God as refuge and strength, and very present help, and defies fear even in the midst of the wildest upheavals. In days when tempests shake loose all solid things, and the restless waters roar and surge till mountains shake, the soul is confident.

The secret of the confidence is the consciousness of the nearness of God. He is a river of gladness in the midst of the city. What matters the tumult around?

The vindication of confidence is to be found in observing His activity in all surrounding things, from this place of safety and strength within the city. The twice repeated refrain (verses 7 and 11) is full of beauty as it reveals the twofold conception of God which is the deepest note in the music. He is the King of all hosts. He is the God of the individual.[1]

G. CAMPBELL MORGAN IN *NOTES ON THE PSALMS*

the devotion of the pilgrim

week
five

PSALM 5

the focus of your devotion

Give ear to my words, O LORD,
consider my sighing.
Listen to my cry for help,
my King and my God,
for to you I pray.
PSALM 5:1-2

Prepare Your Heart

One of the most exciting movies in recent times is *The Gospel According to Matthew*, a visual account of the life of Christ taken word for word from the New International Version of the Bible. In this movie, Jesus actually smiles. Joy is apparent in His life. Love is seen in every move He makes, every word He speaks. As the story unfolds, one is drawn to this Person who gave His life even for those who hated Him.

The story behind the movie is detailed in the book *In the Footsteps of Jesus*, written by Bruce Marchiano, the actor who portrayed Jesus in the film. He is often asked what it was like to play Jesus. As he begins his book, he describes himself as an actor who was "quite simply blown away with the unique and extraordinary experience of portraying Jesus." He goes on to say that as he walked where Jesus walked through the events of His life as described in the gospel of Matthew, he found Jesus to be more than he ever dreamed or hoped He could be and, in the process, he fell in love with Jesus. He says Jesus was a "Man among men."[1]

As you begin this week with the Lord, think about this question: "Who is the object of your devotion?" Two thousand years ago the most extraordinary Person to ever walk the face of this earth lived and laughed and spent time with friends and family. His name is Jesus. His life and purpose is outlined in the Old and New Testaments of the Bible. And He lives today! If you could spend time with Jesus today, would you?

Take some time in preparation for your week to think about what consumes your thoughts in your daily life. How is your life with your God? Do you think about Him often and do you spend time with Him? Write a brief prayer in the space below, asking God to renew your passion for Him.

READ AND STUDY GOD'S WORD

This week, as you think about devotion to God, your example will be David, the man after God's own heart. Psalm 5, written by David, is a "morning prayer" and was probably written during a time of danger (see verses 4-5 and 9-10). This psalm speaks of David's deep devotion to God. It will encourage you in your own devotion to God.

1. Christian devotion is a solemn, passionate dedication and exclusive commitment to Jesus Christ in the power of the Holy Spirit. To be devoted to God implies commitment, loyalty, fidelity, respect, passion, and exclusive attachment. Read Psalm 5 and record what you notice about David's devotion to God.

2. What actions by David demonstrate his devotion to God?

3. In the last days God has spoken to us by His Son, Jesus, who is "the radiance of God's glory and the exact representation of his being" (Hebrews 1:1-3). We can learn much about devotion to God by looking at the actions of those around Jesus during His life on earth. And we can mirror these actions in our own love relationship with Him now. Look at the following three events in the life of Jesus and describe the devotion that is apparent in each one.

Matthew 4:18–5:1

Matthew 14:22-36

Matthew 26:6-13

4. Why were people drawn to Jesus? What do you think it was about Him that caused them to follow Him wherever He went and listen to Him when He spoke? You may look at the following verses for insight into these questions: Matthew 7:28-29; 9:35-36; 15:32; 23:37; John 15:9; 17:23. Record your thoughts below.

Adore God in Prayer

If Jesus were to walk into your room, what would you say to Him? Today imagine that you are sitting with Jesus. Though you cannot see Him with your physical eyes, He is with you even now. Talk to Him, knowing that He is right there with you. Pour out to Him all that is on your heart. You may wish to close your eyes to shut out the world and simply focus on your Lord.

Yield Yourself to God

Jesus does not yearn for works, even though they are important and should be done through love of Him. He longs for a love that is concentrated upon Jesus Himself; it bestows gifts upon Him lavishly; it brings Him sacrifices; it is concerned about Jesus Himself. . . . While He was in Bethany before His passion, He had also looked for love. There He found someone who sympathized with Him and understood how heavy His heart was, because the time had come for Him to begin His road of sorrows. This was Mary. Her love had shown her how deeply grieved was His soul, and she did what she could do for Him. Her entire concern was to comfort and refresh Him. . . . A bridegroom always waits for his bride to come to him so that He can carry on a dialogue of love with her. Jesus is yearning to have fellowship with us and to hear words of love drop from our lips. He is waiting for us. He wants us to be close to Him. He wants to speak to us in our hearts, to cultivate love's intimate relationship with us.[2]

BASILEA SCHLINK IN *MY ALL FOR HIM*

Is it not unspeakably delightful to view the Savior in all His offices, and to perceive Him matchless in each—to shift the kaleidoscope, as it were, and to find fresh combinations of peerless graces? In the manger and in eternity, on the cross and on His throne, in the garden and in His kingdom, among thieves or in the midst of cherubim, He is everywhere "altogether lovely."' Examine carefully every little act of His life, and every trait of His character, and He is as lovely in the minute as in the majestic. Judge Him as you will, you cannot censure; weigh Him as you please, and He will not be found wanting. Eternity shall not discover the shadow of a spot in our Beloved, but rather, as ages revolve, His hidden glories shall shine forth with yet more inconceivable splendor, and His unutterable loveliness shall more and more ravish all celestial minds.[3]

CHARLES SPURGEON IN *MORNING AND EVENING*

How intimate is your love relationship with your Lord? Have you fallen in love with Jesus?

ENJOY HIS PRESENCE

What have you learned about devotion to God today from David's example and the examples in the New Testament? In what ways can you express devotion to your Lord today?

REST IN HIS LOVE

"He who loves me will be loved by my Father, and I too will love him and show myself to him" (John 14:21).

the time of your devotion

In the morning, O LORD, you hear my voice;
in the morning I lay my requests before you
and wait in expectation.
PSALM 5:3

Prepare Your Heart

When does devotion begin and how long does it last? George Mueller, a busy pastor of more than 1,200 believers and a founder of five orphanages, discovered the importance of quiet time with God early in his life with Him. He said, "I have always made it a rule never to begin work till I have had a good season with God. The vigor of our spiritual life will be in exact proportion to the place held by the Word in our life and thoughts." Hudson Taylor, the founder of the China Inland Mission, would rise at 5 A.M. for Bible study and prayer and would often spend two hours a day with God.[1]

While devotion to God is an ongoing relationship of intimacy, joy, and worship, it also includes specific times of communion with Him. This is evidenced not only in the lives of great men and women of God but also in the life of Jesus, who "often withdrew to lonely places and prayed" (Luke 5:16). Why do we need time with God? That is the subject of our study today. As you prepare for your time alone with God today, meditate on these words by Amy Carmichael in *Toward Jerusalem*.

My Quietness

O Thou Who art my quietness, my deep repose,
My rest from strife of tongues, my holy hill,
Fair is Thy pavilion, where I hold me still.

Back let them fall from me, my clamorous foes,
Confusions multiplied;
From crowding things of sense I flee, and in Thee hide.
Until this tyranny be overpast,
Thy hand will hold me fast;
What though the tumult of the storm increase,
Grant to Thy servant strength, O Lord, and bless with peace.[2]

READ AND STUDY GOD'S WORD

1. It is apparent as one reads the psalms of David that this man spent much time alone with God. Read Psalm 5 again and record any additional insights about David, his life of devotion, and what he gained from his time with God. What did he know about God?

2. In Psalm 5, David laid out his requests before God early in the morning. His other psalms reveal that he spent more than just the morning with God. Look at the following verses and record what you learn about David's time with God:

Psalm 6:6

Psalm 8:3-4

Psalm 16:7-8

Psalm 27:4

Psalm 55:16-17

Psalm 57:1-2

3. The Bible teaches that the greatest thing in all of life is to know God. In fact, Jesus defines eternal life as knowing God and Jesus Christ (see John 17:3). When you think about Jesus and His life on earth, what do you think influenced His twelve disciples more than anything else? Who He was as a person. And how could they know Him except that they spent time with Him? Look at Matthew 14:15-33 and record what you see about the quality of their time with Jesus and what they learned about Jesus. Try to imagine that you are there with Jesus, and immerse yourself in the drama of the moment.

The quality of the disciples' time with Jesus

The character of Jesus

ADORE GOD IN PRAYER

Turn to your Prayer Pages in the back of this book. Record any new requests for you, your family, and your friends. Lay each request before the Lord, knowing that He hears and answers. He desires so much to hear your voice. Also, review your previous requests and record any answers to your prayers. After you lay your requests before the Lord, will you, like David, wait in expectation for Him to act?

YIELD YOURSELF TO GOD

Jesus—the son of a peasant girl and a laborer. Jesus—a man who didn't even have a home to call His own. Jesus—who hung out with prostitutes, thieves, cripples, and even a few fishermen. Jesus—a man who was more interested in matters of the heart than anything else. Jesus—a seemingly common, young, small-town man: sleeves rolled up, hair tossed and tumbled by a gust of first-century wind, face tanned and weathered, rough and calloused hands, dirt under the fingernails, soiled feet in well-worn sandals. Jesus—sweat glistening on the brow, creases framing gentle eyes—eyes that look deep into your soul and inescapably breathe "I love you" with every glance. And a smile—oh, what a smile—as big as the sun, beaming at you and you alone as if you're the only person on the entire planet. *Jesus.*[3]

BRUCE MARCHIANO FROM *IN THE FOOTSTEPS OF JESUS*

How well do you know Jesus? If you could spend time today with Jesus, would you?

ENJOY HIS PRESENCE

Think about what you have learned today about your time with God. When is the best time for you to be alone with God? Have you set aside time to be with Him? What will help you to have quality time with Him? Sometime this week, do something special with your Lord, such as breakfast with Him or a walk.

REST IN HIS LOVE

"How great is the love the Father has lavished on us, that we should be called children of God! And that is what we are!" (1 John 3:1).

the place of your devotion

But I, by your great mercy, will come into your house;
in reverence will I bow down toward your holy temple.
PSALM 5:7

Prepare Your Heart

The goal of your time with the Lord today is to think about the atmosphere and surroundings of your daily quiet time. Where do you spend your daily time with God? And what materials do you use in your quiet time? Do you have a variety of resources to allow spontaneity as you sit alone with the Lord each day? The pilgrim of God is aware of the need for a quiet place to be silent and still before the Lord. As you draw near to God this day, meditate on the words of this beloved hymn by Cleland McAfee.

Near to the Heart of God

There is a place of quiet rest, near to the heart of God;
A place where sin cannot molest, near to the heart of God.
There is a place of comfort sweet, near to the heart of God;
A place where we our Savior meet, near to the heart of God.
There is a place of full release, near to the heart of God;
A place where all is joy and peace, near to the heart of God.

Refrain:
O Jesus, blest Redeemer, sent from the heart of God,
Hold us, who wait before Thee, near to the heart of God.

READ AND STUDY GOD'S WORD

David's favorite place to be with God was in God's house. The temple was the place where the Lord's presence dwelt. David loved to be in God's house because He loved to be in God's presence. In Psalm 27:4 David said, "One thing I ask of the LORD, this is what I seek: that I may dwell in the house of the LORD all the days of my life, to gaze upon the beauty of the LORD and to seek him in his temple."

1. Turn to Psalm 5:7 and record everything you notice about David's worship of the Lord. Where and how does he worship?

2. Another example for the Christian pilgrim is the Lord Jesus Christ Himself. When the disciples walked across the countryside with Him, they could never be certain what would happen from day to day. However, Jesus had a habit of spending time with God. Look at the following verses and record what you notice about Jesus' devotional life:

Matthew 14:22-24

Mark 1:35

Luke 4:42-43

Luke 5:15-16

Luke 6:12-13

Luke 9:18,28-29

John 6:14-15

3. What is your most significant insight about Jesus' devotional life?

4. What conditions did Jesus find necessary for His time with God?

ADORE GOD IN PRAYER

Perhaps today you need to hear the words of Jesus: "Come with me by yourselves to a quiet place" (Mark 6:31). Find a quiet place and talk with your Lord. Tell Him everything on your heart. As David did, lay your requests before Him. Ask Him the questions that no one can seem to answer. Don't be afraid to dream big dreams and ask the Lord for the impossible. Perhaps that dream deep in your heart was placed there by the Lord. If it's His dream, He will make it live. Maybe He will change your heart. Lay before Him the sin that keeps nagging your heart. Remember, God's Word says, "If we confess our sins, he is faithful and just and will forgive us our sins and purify us from all unrighteousness" (1 John 1:9).

As you talk with the Lord, keep your Bible open. Sometimes He will bring a verse to mind. Turn to that verse, and think long and hard about what it says. Ask the Lord to speak to you from His Word. Turn to God's promises as you talk with Him, and read them out loud. Keep your Journal open to write any insights, ideas, or prayers as you sit with the Lord. Thank God that He hears when you speak and actually delights in your company. He loves to be with you.

YIELD YOURSELF TO GOD

Dr. Donald S. Whitney devotes an entire chapter to the subject of "Silence and Solitude" in his book *Spiritual Disciplines for the Christian Life*. In that chapter he speaks of the necessity of silence and solitude in our lives.

There is something both appealing and transforming about silence and solitude. Other than Jesus Christ, perhaps the greatest men under each Covenant—Moses and the

Apostle Paul—were both transformed through years of virtual isolation in a remote wilderness. . . . There is a part of our spirit that craves silence and solitude. Just as we must engage with others for some of the Disciplines of the Christian life, so there are times when we must temporarily withdraw into the Disciplines of silence and solitude. . . . We all need times to unstring the bow of our routine stresses and enjoy the restoration that silence and solitude can provide for our body and soul.[1]

ENJOY HIS PRESENCE

Have you found a quiet place with your Lord? Will you, as a pilgrim of God, make a commitment to set aside the time and find a quiet place so that you might become intimate with Him? Record this commitment in a prayer to the Lord in your Journal.

REST IN HIS LOVE

"But when you pray, go into your room, close the door and pray to your Father, who is unseen. Then your Father, who sees what is done in secret, will reward you" (Matthew 6:6).

the substance of your devotion

But let all who take refuge in you be glad;
let them ever sing for joy.
Spread your protection over them,
that those who love your name may rejoice in you.
PSALM 5:11

Prepare Your Heart

What does it take for a pilgrim of God to have a rich life of devotion? What qualities are essential to the pilgrim if he or she would enjoy intimacy with God? He or she needs a heart fixed on God and knowing Him. Have you resolved in your heart to know God?

Jim Elliot was one such saint who was single-minded about pursuing this goal. His frequent prayer while attending Wheaton College was, "O God, my heart is fixed."[1] He set his alarm clock every night so he would wake in time to meet with God for prayer and study of His Word.

Elliot's heart was aflame with love for Jesus Christ. He was recklessly abandoned to the will of God. He said, "He is no fool who gives what he cannot keep to gain what he cannot lose."[2] In fact, as a missionary in Ecuador, he ultimately was martyred for his faith in Christ. However, the story of his unique life with God and his commitment to Jesus Christ has inspired many who have become missionaries around the world. His rich devotional life has inspired many to draw near to God.

The substance of your devotion to God is its essential quality. It may be rich and ardent or lackluster and boring. The intimacy of your relationship with God is what determines this quality of devotion. While intimacy with God and quality of devotion are somewhat interdependent, your intimacy with God is a gift of His grace and rests wholly on Him as the Giver of Himself. Yet He does promise that those who seek Him will find Him (see Jeremiah 29:13). In Psalm 5, the text for your study, the substance of David's devotion is joy and love for God. These two qualities are the foundation of a rich inner life with God. They grow from within as you spend time with Him. They are not of this world and cannot be manufactured on demand. They are supernatural and come from the presence of God in your life.

David, God's pilgrim, determined to draw near to God and find refuge in Him. In doing so, he found himself face to face with the living God. The result was gladness of heart, joy, rejoicing, and love for God. David also hated evil because of his great love for God (see Psalm 5:8-10). The same thing happened to the earliest followers of the Lord Jesus Christ. As they looked into His eyes and sensed His compassion, forgiveness, and love, their lives were forever changed. Out of their dynamic relationships with Jesus, they developed a passionate and ardent love for Him.

Today you are going to have the opportunity to meditate on the lives of two biblical characters who had rich inner lives with God. As you begin your quiet time, think about the last six months of your life. Describe your devotional life with God. What do you desire in your relationship with the Lord? Write a prayer to Him in your Journal.

READ AND STUDY GOD'S WORD

1. Turn to Psalm 5 and write out verse 11, word for word.

2. What does the psalmist observe about the lives of those who take refuge in God?

3. The Bible records numerous events that portray a rich devotional life with God. Look at the following encounters with God, and record what you notice about the quality of devotion in each life:

Exodus 33:7—34:10

2 Samuel 6:12-23

4. Describe in your own words what it means to have a rich devotional life with God. Do you define it in terms of activities or in terms of relationship? And then, how do disciplines such as journaling, devotional reading, Bible study, and prayer fit into your devotional life?

5. What have you learned that will help you in your own devotional life with God?

ADORE GOD IN PRAYER

The psalms contain many expressions of praise and love for God. These psalms can help you in the quality of your devotion. Psalms 145–150 are filled with words of praise, joy, and love for God. Turn to these psalms and pray at least one of them to God, personalizing them in your own words. This is not simply an exercise, for you are using the living and active Word of God. You will find that God's Word will begin to fill your heart, heal your soul, and turn your gaze to the Lord.

YIELD YOURSELF TO GOD

Do you know, beyond all doubt, that you are God's own child and you are loved by Him without measure? It is true. Your soul is loved, with a love so tender, by the One who is highest of all. His is a love so wonderful, far beyond anything we created beings can fully fathom. No one, in this life, can know how passionately the Creator longs for us. Enter into this love, then, by His empowering grace. Be diligent as you go to prayer. Still the nagging, worrying voices that tell you to doubt your Lover's complete trustworthiness—and fix your thoughts on His good, lofty, and limitless compassion—so that you remain in His love. Trust Him. Learn what it means to hide your soul in Him in this way, in utter trust. After that, your prayers will be filled with true reverence—that is, a joyful respect not mixed with resentment, demands, or bargaining. For then our natural will is to have God himself—nothing less. And God's good will is simply to have us. To wrap us in himself, and in eternal life. Never stop willing or loving, until you are united with Him in happy completeness. . . . This is the sturdy foundation on which everything else in your spiritual life depends, now and forever.[3]

JULIAN OF NORWICH IN *I PROMISE YOU A CROWN*

Is your devotional life characterized by love for God and joy in Him? Is the Lord your greatest treasure? Is there anything in your life that takes first place in your life instead of the Lord Jesus Christ? Write a simple prayer of love, commitment, and devotion to your Lord in your Journal.

ENJOY HIS PRESENCE

Music has been called "the foretaste of eternal life." Notice that the psalmist sings for joy. Consider including music in your quiet time. There are many ways to do this. You might play music that leads you to worship God. Or you may get a book of hymns or praise songs and sing one each morning in your quiet time. This week, include music in your quiet time at least once. Then record in your Journal the influence of the music on your heart. How did it affect the quality of your devotion to God?

REST IN HIS LOVE

"The joy of the LORD is your strength" (Nehemiah 8:10).

the result of your devotion

For surely, O LORD, you bless the righteous;
you surround them with your favor as with a shield.
PSALM 5:12

Prepare Your Heart

In the film *Chariots of Fire*, Olympic runner Eric Liddell says the memorable words, "When I run, I feel His pleasure." Liddell had a passion for God and weighed his actions, words, and thoughts before God each morning in his quiet time. Others described him as someone who "completely surrendered his life to God and who lived what he himself described as a God-controlled life."[1] He was thought to be the most Christlike individual they had ever met. His love for Christ caused him to take a stand when asked to run on the Lord's Day (Sunday) in the 1924 Olympics. He simply said, "I'm not running." Liddell's decision to honor the Lord and not compromise his convictions was a powerful encouragement to the Christians of his day.

What many do not know is that Liddell became a missionary to China and in 1943 was captured and placed in a Japanese internment camp. He arose early every morning, studied his Bible, and brought cheer and comfort to others in the camp. He spent much time with the children, telling stories and teaching them hymns and principles from God's Word. One child remembers him as the one with the gentle face and the warm smile. While in this internment camp, his health began to deteriorate because of a brain tumor. Just before his death, he asked to hear his favorite hymn:

> Be still, my soul, the Lord is on thy side;
> Bear patiently the cross of grief or pain;
> Leave to thy God to order and provide;
> In every change He faithful will remain,

Be still, my soul, thy best, thy heavenly Friend
Through thorny ways leads to a joyful end.

Eric Liddell died at the age of forty-three in January 1945. His final words, spoken to a camp nurse, were, "It's complete surrender." He knew that he had the great blessings of God. Therefore, he placed his life in God's hands. That is why he could wholeheartedly say, "When I run, I feel His pleasure."

When you journey through life as God's pilgrim, do you sense your Lord's pleasure? Do you know that you have the smile of God? In Psalm 5, David's final words speak of the result of your devotion. You will be blessed by God and surrounded by His favor. This was the experience of Eric Liddell and the great testimony of his life.

However, what does that mean? Does it mean that you will never have another problem or that you will gain material wealth and success? There is a false notion circulating in the church that when good things happen, God is blessing us, and when bad things happen, then we are in the position of hoping that God will soon bless us again by changing our circumstances. Jesus taught that those who are poor in spirit and who mourn are blessed. No wonder the crowds flocked to be near Him. They were not wealthy. They experienced pain and brokenness. And they knew they were not nearly as religious as the Pharisees were. The issue is not that wealth is wrong and poverty and brokenness are preferred. No, it is just that those things are not a measure of God's blessing. What does it mean to be blessed by God? That is the subject of your time with Him today. Ask God to quiet your heart that you may hear Him speak today.

READ AND STUDY GOD'S WORD

The Greek word for blessing is *makarios*. It means to possess God's favor and therefore to experience fulfillment and satisfaction, not because of positive circumstances but because of Christ's presence in one's life. The blessed person is "in the world yet independent of the world; his satisfaction comes from God and not from favorable circumstances."[2] This is a description of the pilgrim of God.

This week you have seen that the pilgrim's devotion to God is devotion to a Person and not a religion. Your gaze has been filled with the character of Jesus Christ. And now, what is the result of your devotion? The result is God's blessings, which can be summed up in one phrase: the smile of God seen in Jesus Christ. Hebrews 1:1-3 tells us that God has spoken in Jesus. When others came near Jesus and looked into His face, how do you think Jesus looked at them in return? Was it with a stern, angry, demanding response? In His eyes, others saw God's overwhelming love and compassion, and it was more than they could imagine. It surprised them. And it blessed them.

That is what happens when you turn to God and draw near to Him in devotion. You discover that He is a God of compassion and that He will not cast you away. That is why the Lord invites you to "cast all your anxiety on him because He cares for you" (1 Peter 5:7). In the final summary of life, God will be the source of satisfaction in the depths of your heart. He is the one Who lasts forever, even when heaven and earth pass away. Nothing can separate you from His love. That is why His blessings are independent of circumstances. You can still experience Him even in the darkest of nights.

1. To understand God's blessings, the result of your devotion, turn to the following verses. Spend time with each one and record your insights about God's blessings in the spaces provided. Who is blessed, and what are some of God's blessings?

Matthew 5:1-12

John 12:12-15

John 13:13-17

John 20:29

James 1:12

1 Peter 3:13-15

1 Peter 4:14

Revelation 1:3

Revelation 22:14

2. In Ephesians 1, Paul outlines some of the ways you, as God's pilgrim, have been blessed. Read Ephesians 1:3-14 and record what you learn.

ADORE GOD IN PRAYER

One day Jesus was on the way to Jerusalem, traveling on the border between Samaria and Galilee. As He was entering a village, ten men who had leprosy stood at a distance and cried out, "Jesus, Master, have mercy on us!" (Luke 17:13, NASB). And Jesus, in His mercy and compassion, healed all ten of those men. Imagine how their lives were changed! Then the ten men walked away from Jesus. One of them, when he saw he was healed, came back, praising God in a loud voice. He threw himself at Jesus' feet and thanked Him.

This week you have learned many truths about your life with God. And today you have seen the result: blessing from God. Take time now to turn to the Lord and thank Him for how He has blessed you. You might want to take a page in your Journal and title it "Blessings." List those things for which you are thankful.

YIELD YOURSELF TO GOD

Abraham possessed nothing. Yet was not this poor man rich! Everything he had owned before was his still to enjoy: sheep, camels, herds, and goods of every sort. He had also his wife and his friends, and best of all he had his son Isaac safe by his side. He had everything, *but he possessed nothing*. There is the spiritual secret. There is the sweet theology of the heart which can be learned only in the school of renunciation. The books on systematic theology overlook this, but the wise will understand.[3]

A. W. TOZER IN THE PURSUIT OF GOD

Do you know this blessedness of possessing nothing so that Christ might mean everything to you?

ENJOY HIS PRESENCE

Father, I want to know Thee, but my cowardly heart fears to give up its toys. I cannot part with them without inward bleeding, and I do not try to hide from Thee the terror of the parting. I come trembling, but I do come. Please root from my heart all those things which I have cherished so long and which have become a very part of my living self, so that Thou mayest enter and dwell there without a rival. Then shalt Thou make the place of Thy feet glorious. Then shall my heart have no need of the sun to shine in it, for Thyself wilt be the light of it, and there shall be no night there. In Jesus' name, Amen.[4]

A. W. TOZER IN THE PURSUIT OF GOD

REST IN HIS LOVE

"His divine power has given us everything we need for life and godliness through our knowledge of him who called us by his own glory and goodness" (2 Peter 1:3).

Dear Friend,

Take these two days to reflect on everything you have learned from Psalm 5, written by David, the man after God's own heart. In fact, as you read through this psalm, you may notice something new. Record your insights in your Journal. Reflect on your life of devotion with God and ask Him to enrich your quiet times. You may wish to look through the introduction to this study and think about the many disciplines of devotion, such as journaling, devotional reading, Bible study, prayer, worship, silence, and solitude. Is there something new to you, such as journaling, that you might try to incorporate in your quiet times?

Review your quiet times this week and take note of your most significant insights. Record your favorite insight, the page of your favorite quote, and your favorite verses from your time with the Lord this week.

Your most significant insight

Your favorite quote

Your favorite verse

Verse 12: A shield, in war, guards only one side, but the favor of God is to the saints a defense on every side; like the hedge about Job, round about so that, while they keep themselves under the divine protection, they are entirely safe and ought to be entirely satisfied.[1]

MATTHEW HENRY IN *MATTHEW HENRY'S COMMENTARY*

The secret of a close relationship with God is to pray to Him earnestly each morning. In the morning, our minds are more free from problems and then we can commit the whole day to God. Regular communication helps any friendship and is certainly necessary for a strong relationship with God. We need to communicate with Him daily. Do you have a regular time to pray and read God's Word?[2]

FROM THE *LIFE APPLICATION BIBLE*

Sometimes we are in such distress that our prayers are only desperate cries for God to help us. At still other times we cannot find words adequate to express our feelings or voice what we need, though we are nevertheless still praying. But here is the encouraging thing: God hears all kinds of prayers.[3]

JAMES MONTGOMERY BOICE IN *PSALMS*

In the same way, the Spirit helps us in our weakness. We do not know what we ought to pray for, but the Spirit himself intercedes for us with groans that words cannot express. And he who searches our hearts knows the mind of the Spirit, because the Spirit intercedes for the saints in accordance with God's will.

ROMANS 8:26-27

the prayer of the pilgrim

week
six

PSALM 107

the foundation of your prayer

Give thanks to the LORD, for he is good;
his love endures forever. . . .
Consider the great love of the LORD.
PSALM 107:1,43

Prepare Your Heart

What is the paramount spiritual issue in the world today? It is not astrology, the New Age, or even the Bible, but prayer. *Life* magazine highlighted the topic in an issue entitled "The Power of Prayer: How Americans Talk to God." Nine out of ten Americans told *Life* they pray frequently and earnestly, and almost all said God had answered their prayers.

There are many perspectives about prayer and how it fits into our life. What do you believe about prayer? If God is all-knowing and sovereign, then why pray? Do your prayers really make any difference? What is prayer, and how do you do it? This week you will have the opportunity to think about what prayer means. What you believe is going to make the difference in your life of prayer.

When the people of Israel were freed from their captivity in Babylon and allowed to return to Jerusalem, they had many reasons to thank God. During this time, Psalm 107 was written as a hymn of thanksgiving, celebrating God's deliverances in answer to their prayers. If ever the people of Israel had been in distress, it was when Jerusalem was destroyed and they were deported to Babylon. From their place of captivity, they cried out to God. In God's time, He delivered them and brought them back to their land. That is the context of Psalm 107. From this psalm you will learn some important principles about prayer. For surely, if ever God delivered in response to the prayers of His people, it was during the Babylonian captivity.

As you begin your quiet times this week, take a few moments to consider the place of prayer in your life. Would you consider yourself a prayer warrior? Or is prayer a rare occasion in your relationship with God? Record your thoughts in your Journal. Then draw near to God and pray, "Lord, teach [me] to pray" (Luke 11:1).

READ AND STUDY GOD'S WORD

1. Read through Psalm 107, keeping in mind that this is a psalm of thanksgiving for God's deliverances in answer to His people's prayers. Record your first impressions of this psalm.

2. Today you are going to look at the foundation of all prayer. Read Psalm 107 again and record everything you learn about God.

3. In this psalm you see that the foundation of your prayers is the character of God. In fact, the greatest result of prayer is a deeper knowledge of His character and a more intimate fellowship with Him. The most important aspect of His character in relation to prayer is His goodness and love (see Psalm 107:1,43). If He is not good and does not love, then our prayers may fall on deaf or uninterested ears. Because He is good and all-loving, then we can cry out to Him in our trouble and know that His answer will be the very best and in accordance with His will. Because of His goodness, He can be trusted in full surrender. So today, for further study, "consider the great love of the LORD" (Psalm 107:43). Look at the following verses and record what you learn about God's love and goodness:

God's Love

Psalm 147:11

John 3:16

1 John 3:1; 4:7-10

God's Goodness
Psalm 31:19-21

Psalm 100:5

Psalm 145:8-9

4. Jesus revealed God's love and goodness by telling others something very important about Himself. Turn to John 10:11-18. After reading this passage, record your insights about Jesus.

5. What significance do Jesus' words have for you? How do they make a difference in your life of prayer?

6. What difference does it make to you that God loves you and is good?

7. How does knowing God loves you and is good make a difference in your prayers?

ADORE GOD IN PRAYER

One of the best ways to learn to pray is to hear others pray. This week you will have the opportunity to pray through some of the psalms and the prayers of men and women who knew and loved God. Use their words to lead you into your own prayer. As you pray, take note of the words that impress your heart the most.

> Heavenly Father, I pray that Jesus Christ may become dearer to me. May I love him as a personal friend and hide myself in the hourly awareness of his presence. May I have no taste or desire for things which he would disapprove. Let his love constrain me not to live for myself, but for him.[1]
>
> F. B. MEYER IN DAILY PRAYERS

> Show me your ways, O LORD,
> teach me your paths;
> guide me in your truth and teach me,
> for you are God my Savior,
> and my hope is in you all day long.
> Remember, O Lord, your great mercy and love,
> for they are from of old.
> Remember not the sins of my youth
> and my rebellious ways;
> according to your love remember me,
> for you are good, O LORD.
>
> PSALM 25:4-7 (EMPHASIS ADDED)

YIELD YOURSELF TO GOD

> It will be as impossible for a good God to cast us off as it would be for a good mother to cast off her child. We may be in trouble and darkness, and may feel as if we were cast off and forsaken, but our feelings have nothing to do with the facts, and the fact is that God is good, and could not do it. The good Shepherd does not cast off the sheep that is lost, and take no further care of it, but He goes out to seek for it, and He

seeks until He finds it. . . . A great many things in God's divine providences do not look like goodness to the eye of sense, and in reading the Psalms we wonder perhaps how the psalmist could say, after some of the things he records, *for his mercy endureth forever.* But faith sits down before mysteries such as these, and says, "The Lord is good, therefore all that He does must be good, no matter how it looks, and I can wait for His explanations."

HANNAH WHITALL SMITH IN *THE GOD OF ALL COMFORT*

In *The Knowledge of the Holy,* A. W. Tozer points out that God's goodness is always the ground of our expectation and that His love is a pillar on which our hope rests.[2] Have you discovered, in knowing the love and goodness of God, the courage and the faith to pray?

ENJOY HIS PRESENCE

Nobody is wholly satisfied with himself. Our lives are made up of lights and shadows, of some good days and many unsatisfactory days. We have learned that the good days and hours come when we are very close to Christ, and that the poor days come whenever we push Him out of our thoughts. Clearly, then, the way to a more consistent high level is to take Him into everything we do or say or think.[3]

FRANK LAUBACH IN *MAN OF PRAYER*

What are ways that you can bring God into everything you do or say or think today? Consider using a page in your Journal to keep a record of what God reveals about Himself to you in His Word and in prayer each day.

REST IN HIS LOVE

"Which of you, if his son asks for bread, will give him a stone? Or if he asks for a fish, will give him a snake? If you, then, though you are evil, know how to give good gifts to your children, how much more will your Father in heaven give good gifts to those who ask him!" (Matthew 7:9-11).

the definition of prayer

Let the redeemed of the LORD say this . . .
PSALM 107:2

Prepare Your Heart

What is the prayer of the pilgrim? One man defined it like no other: with his life. In the 1800s lived a man of prayer, E. M. Bounds. Bounds made it a habit to rise at four o'clock in the morning to be alone with the Lord in prayer for three hours. Not only did he live a life of prayer, he also wrote such books as *Power Through Prayer*, *The Essentials of Prayer*, *The Necessity of Prayer*, and *Purpose in Prayer*. Bounds said, "Prayer is the divinely appointed means by which man comes into direct connection with God. . . . Prayer means calling upon God for things we desire, asking things of God. . . . Prayer is revealed as a direct application to God for some temporal or spiritual good. It is an appeal to God to intervene in life's affairs for the good of those for whom we pray."[1]

How would you define prayer? That is your subject of study today. Draw near to God now and ask Him to quiet your heart. Again, pray the disciples' prayer: "Lord, teach us to pray" (Luke 11:1). Meditate on A. W. Tozer's prayer as a preparation of heart: "O God, show me Thy glory, I pray Thee, that so I may know Thee indeed. Begin in mercy a new work of love within me. Say to my soul, 'Rise up, my love, my fair one, and come away.' Then give me grace to rise and follow Thee up from this misty lowland where I have wandered so long. In Jesus' name. Amen."[2]

READ AND STUDY GOD'S WORD

Psalm 107 is directed to a particular group: the redeemed of the Lord. And the exhortation to them is to communicate with the Lord. The psalmist exhorts them to thank the Lord for His goodness and enduring love: "Give thanks to the LORD, for he is good; his love endures forever. Let the redeemed of the LORD say this . . . " (Psalm 107:1-2). How do the redeemed of the Lord speak to their God? What is that peculiar privilege granted to those who belong to the Lord? What is prayer? These are the questions you are going to think about today.

1. Jesus taught many principles of prayer. Perhaps His greatest teaching came in response to His disciples' request, "Lord, teach us to pray" (Luke 11:1). Turn to Luke 11:1-4. Read Jesus' response to His disciples. Compare it to Matthew 6:5-13. After reading these passages, look at the Matthew passage again. Read it line by line, and record what you learn about prayer from each statement.

2. Look at the following verses and record everything you learn from Jesus about prayer:
   Matthew 7:7-11

   Luke 11:5-13

   Luke 18:1-8

   Luke 21:36; 22:44-46

   John 14:12-17

John 15:5-8

3. How would you define *prayer*?

ADORE GOD IN PRAYER

Take some time now and think about what you are learning about prayer. Prayer has been defined in many ways. It is first and foremost communion with God. The word *communion* implies sharing, exchange, cooperation, interaction, rapport, harmony, fellowship, together-ness, companionship, friendship, camaraderie, connectedness, intimacy, familiarity, relation-ship, communication, interchange, dialogue, and conversation. It is private and personal, yet the world sees the results. Prayer is grasping the hand of the One who already holds you in His everlasting arms. In His hand you will find comfort, encouragement, and power as the Resource beyond all resources for your every need.

With that in mind, draw near to God and commune with Him. Begin with silence. Then, with your Bible open to Matthew 6:9-13, pray each line of the Lord's Prayer. Expand on each thought. For example: "Our Father in heaven, hallowed be your name. You are majestic and holy and awesome. Your works are greater than my mind can comprehend." Your words do not need to be lofty or articulate. Speak from your heart to the One who has loved you enough to give what was dearest to Him that you might belong to Him forever.

YIELD YOURSELF TO GOD

Richard Foster shares a story in his book *Prayer: Finding the Heart's True Home*. A father was hav-ing a challenging time with his two-year-old son at a shopping mall. His child would not be quiet or obey. Finally, the father got a brilliant idea. Foster describes it this way:

Under some special inspiration, the father scooped up his son and, holding him close to his chest, began singing an impromptu love song. None of the words rhymed. He sang off key. And yet, as best he could, this father began sharing his heart. "I love you," he sang. "I'm so glad you're my boy. You make me happy. I like the way you laugh." On they went from one store to the next. Quietly the father continued singing off key and making up words that did not rhyme. The child relaxed and became still, listening to this strange and wonderful song. Finally, they finished shopping and went to the car. As the father opened the door and prepared to buckle his son into the car seat, the child lifted his head and said simply, "Sing it to me again, Daddy! Sing it to me again!" Prayer is a little like that. With simplicity of heart we allow ourselves to be gathered up into the arms of the Father and let him sing his love song over us.[3]

Prayer is a sincere, sensible, affectionate, pouring out of the heart or soul to God through Christ, by the strength or assistance of the Spirit.[4]

JOHN BUNYAN IN *PRAYER*

Prayer is the breath of the soul, the organ by which we receive Christ into our parched and withered hearts. . . . All He needs is access. He enters in of His own accord, because He desires to come in. And He enters in wherever He is not denied admittance. . . . God has designed prayer as a means of intimate and joyous fellowship between God and man. . . . To pray is nothing more involved than to let Jesus into our needs. To pray is to give Jesus permission to employ His powers in the alleviation of our distress. To pray is to let Jesus glorify His name in the midst of our needs. . . . To pray is nothing more involved than to open the door, giving Jesus access to our needs and permitting Him to exercise His own power in dealing with them.[5]

O. HALLESBY IN *PRAYER*

ENJOY HIS PRESENCE

What has been your most significant insight about prayer today? How will it make a difference in your prayer life?

REST IN HIS LOVE

"Do not be anxious about anything, but in everything, by prayer and petition, with thanksgiving, present your requests to God. And the peace of God, which transcends all understanding, will guard your hearts and your minds in Christ Jesus" (Philippians 4:6-7).

the necessity of prayer

Some wandered in desert wastelands,
finding no way to a city where they could settle.
They were hungry and thirsty,
and their lives ebbed away.
PSALM 107:4-5

Prepare Your Heart

How does God make a man or a woman of prayer? It is through the school of pilgrimage. What is this school? It is the event that etches in the mind and heart of a man or woman the absolute need for God and the fact that he or she is forever God's pilgrim. It may be a time of change, a time of suffering, or simply a one-time event.

For E. M. Bounds, this life-changing event occurred during the Civil War. Through it he came to understand his helplessness and great need for God. One biographer describes it this way: "If a man considers himself to be an iron pillar, he is of no use to God. God works through broken reeds. Between 1861 and 1865 Bounds became a broken reed."[1]

During the Civil War, Bounds was captured, stripped of all of his belongings and even of his citizenship. He lost everything. He was banished from his home state, and he never again felt at home in any place. After this time, he became a preacher, earned very little salary, had very few possessions, and could not afford to buy a house. He never complained. And more than anything else, he was a man of prayer. God had taught him in his Civil War pilgrimage experience that his only security was in God and that he belonged to God. He knew and understood in the depths of his soul his great need for God.

Today you will have the opportunity to think through the question "Why pray?" In doing so, you, as God's pilgrim, will learn the necessity of prayer. The necessity of prayer is really the necessity of God in your life. As you draw near to God today, think about what you are learning about prayer. Ask God again: "Lord, teach me to pray."

READ AND STUDY GOD'S WORD

The people of Israel were certainly God's pilgrims on His pilgrimage. And God had a high purpose for them that extended far beyond their lifetime. Through God's chosen people, a Messiah would be born who would save His people from their sins. God never abandons His people, even in their great distress. Psalm 107 celebrates God's great deliverances in answer to His people's prayers.

1. Read Psalm 107 again, this time looking for any repeated phrases. Record all repeated phrases here.

2. Did you notice that there are four distinct events marked by the phrase "then they cried out to the LORD in their trouble, and he delivered them from their distress" (Psalm 107:6; see also verses 13,19,28)? Read Psalm 107 and describe these four life situations that might be thought of as "schools of pilgrimage." In each case, why did God's people need to pray?

verses 4-5

verses 10-12

verses 17-18

verses 23-27

3. Other areas of Scripture speak to the necessity of prayer and the need for God. Look at the following verses and record what you learn:
John 15:5,7

Philippians 4:6-7

Romans 8:26-27,34

Hebrews 4:15-16

Hebrews 7:25-26

James 5:13-16

ADORE GOD IN PRAYER

What are your needs today? What are your worries? Will you rely on God? And do you long to know God? Draw near to Him today and make your requests known to Him. You might want to turn to a Prayer Page and record each need. Then, when God answers, you can record how He answered your prayers.

Devotion

God of my end,
It is my greatest, noblest pleasure
to be acquainted with thee
and with my rational, immortal soul;
It is sweet and entertaining
to look into my being
when all my powers and passions
are united and engaged in pursuit of thee,
when my soul longs and passionately breathes after conformity to thee
and the full enjoyment of thee;

No hours pass away with so much pleasure
as those spent in communion with thee
and with my heart.
O how desirable, how profitable to the Christian life
is a spirit of holy watchfulness
and godly jealousy over myself.
When my soul is afraid of nothing
except grieving and offending thee, the blessed God,
my Father and friend,
whom I then love and long to please,
rather than be happy in myself!
Knowing, as I do, that this is *the* pious temper,
worthy of the highest ambition, and closest pursuit
of intelligent creatures and holy Christians,
may my joy derive from glorifying and delighting thee.
I long to fill all my time for thee,
whether at home or in the way;
to place all my concerns in thy hands;
to be entirely at thy disposal,
having no will or interest of my own.
Help me to live to thee forever,
to make thee my last and only end,
so that I may never more in one instance love my sinful self.[2]

FROM *THE VALLEY OF VISION: A COLLECTION OF PURITAN PRAYERS AND DEVOTIONS*

YIELD YOURSELF TO GOD

Be not anxious because of your helplessness. Above all, do not let it prevent you from praying. Helplessness is the real secret and the impelling power of prayer. You should therefore rather try to thank God for the feeling of helplessness which He has given you. It is one of the greatest gifts which God can impart to us. For it is only when we are helpless that we open our hearts to Jesus and let Him help us in our distress, according to His grace and mercy. . . . I never grow weary of emphasizing our helplessness, for it is the decisive factor not only in our prayer life, but in our whole relationship to God. As long as we are conscious of our helplessness we will not be overtaken by any difficulty, disturbed by any distress or frightened by any hindrance. We will expect nothing of ourselves and therefore bring all our difficulties and hindrances to God in prayer. And this means to open the door unto Him and to give God the opportunity to help us in our helplessness by means of the miraculous powers which are at His disposal.[3]

O. HALLESBY IN *PRAYER*

The spirit of a pilgrim greatly facilitates praying. An earth-bound, earth-satisfied spirit cannot pray. In such a heart, the flame of spiritual desire is either gone out or smouldering in faintest glow. The wings of its faith are clipped, its eyes are filmed, its tongue silenced. But they, who in unswerving faith and unceasing prayer wait continually upon the Lord, *do* renew their strength, *do* mount up with wings as eagles, *do* run and are not weary, *do* walk and not faint.[4]

E. M. BOUNDS IN *THE NECESSITY OF PRAYER*

ENJOY HIS PRESENCE

What school of pilgrimage has God taken you through that has shown you your great need of prayer and God in your own life? What have you learned today that encourages you to pray? Will you pray?

REST IN HIS LOVE

"For the eyes of the LORD move to and fro throughout the earth that He may strongly support those whose heart is completely His" (2 Chronicles 16:9, NASB).

the practice of prayer

Then they cried out to the LORD in their trouble,
and he delivered them from their distress.
PSALM 107:6

Prepare Your Heart

You have seen your need to pray. Now how do you pray? What does it involve? E. M. Bounds discipled one young man in the practice of prayer and "taught him to pray early and earnestly, asking God to give him the essential ingredients for a meaningful prayer life. These essentials included faith, trust, desire, fervency, persistence, good character and conduct, obedience, and vigilance."[1] Each man or woman of God has expressed his or her life of prayer in a unique way based upon each individual's relationship with God. There are many ways to pray, including praying Scripture, singing, writing prayers in a journal, personalizing the Psalms, conversing with God, silence and solitude, listening and waiting on God, and writing out prayer requests. How can you enrich your own prayer life? Draw near to God and once again pray that wonderful prayer: "Lord, teach me to pray."

READ AND STUDY GOD'S WORD

Today you will look at several aspects of the practice of prayer: the exhortation to pray, kinds of prayer, and examples of those who prayed.

The Exhortation to Pray

1. God encourages His pilgrims to pray. Look at the following verses and record what you learn:

Colossians 4:2

1 Thessalonians 5:17

Kinds of Prayers

2. There are many kinds of prayers in the Word of God. Look at the following verses to learn about some of the most important ways to pray:

James 5:15 (intercession)

Ephesians 6:18 (petition)

1 Timothy 2:1-3 (supplication)

Psalm 5:3 (requests)

1 John 1:9 (confession)

Psalm 25:5 (waiting and hoping)

Psalm 77:11-12 (remembering and meditating on God and His ways)

Psalm 148:1 (praise and worship)

Examples of Prayer

3. The following are examples of prayers in the Bible. *Choose one example* and record your
most significant insights. If you have more time, look at more of these examples of
prayer. What can you learn that will help you in your own prayers?
   Ezra 9:1–10:12 (Ezra praying for the revival of his people)

John 17:1-26 (Jesus praying for His disciples)

Matthew 26:36-44 (Jesus praying in His great hour of need)

Ephesians 1:18-19; 3:14-21 (Paul praying for the church at Ephesus)

Philippians 1:9-11 (Paul praying for the church at Philippi)

Colossians 1:9-12 (Paul praying for the church at Colossae)

4. Summarize in two or three sentences what you have learned about how to pray.

Adore God in Prayer

Think about what you have learned today about prayer. Choose one of the examples of prayer, such as Paul's, Ezra's, or Jesus' prayers, and pray the words for yourself and others. You might consider taking a page in your Journal and writing out the words as a prayer to God, personalizing them for your own life.

Yield Yourself to God

> What really gives prayer its power is that I take God's thoughts from his Word and present them before Him. Then I am enabled to pray according to God's Word. How indispensable God's Word is for all true prayer.[2]
>
> ANDREW MURRAY IN *GOD'S BEST SECRETS*

> There is no more useful tool to get us into prayer than God's precious Word. If we will read it, pray it, and practice it, the Word will motivate us into prayer. As we use the Scriptures to aid our praying, we will discover them to be God's chosen textbook on prayer. Praying the Scriptures instructs us in prayer that is pleasing to God, productive for us and powerful in its outreach.[3]
>
> JUDSON CORNWALL IN *PRAYING THE SCRIPTURES*

> One of the most useful things is to vocalize your prayers. This does not mean they have to be so loud that they become a distraction to others, or worse, a kind of pious showing off. It simply means you articulate your prayers, moving your lips perhaps; the energy devoted to expressing your thoughts in words and sentences will order and discipline your mind, and help deter meandering. Another thing you can do is pray over the Scriptures. . . . In other words, it is entirely appropriate to tie your praying to your Bible reading. . . . Whatever the reading scheme, it is essential to read the passage slowly and thoughtfully so as to retrieve at least some of its meaning and bearing on your life. Those truths and entailments can be the basis of a great deal of reflective praying. . . . Praying through the worship sections of the better hymnals can prove immensely edifying and will certainly help you to focus your mind and heart in one

direction for a while. . . . One senior saint I know has long made it his practice to pray through the Lord's Prayer, thinking through the implications of each petition as he goes, and organizing his prayers around those implications. . . . Many others make prayer lists of various sorts. . . . This may be part of the discipline of what has come to be called "journaling."[4]

D. A. CARSON IN A CALL TO SPIRITUAL REFORMATION

How will you pray today?

ENJOY HIS PRESENCE

I Need Thee Every Hour

I need thee every hour, most gracious Lord;
No tender voice like thine can peace afford.

Refrain:
I need thee, O I need thee;
Every hour I need thee!
O bless me now, my Savior—
I come to thee.

I need thee every hour, stay thou nearby;
Temptations lose their power, when thou art nigh.

I need thee every hour, in joy or pain;
Come quickly, and abide, or life is vain.

I need thee every hour, teach me thy will,
And thy rich promises in me fulfill.

ANNIE S. HAWKS AND ROBERT LOWRY

REST IN HIS LOVE

"And pray in the Spirit on all occasions with all kinds of prayers and requests. With this in mind, be alert and always keep on praying for all the saints" (Ephesians 6:18).

"Be joyful always; pray continually; give thanks in all circumstances, for this is God's will for you in Christ Jesus" (1 Thessalonians 5:16-18).

the power in prayer

He led them by a straight way
to a city where they could settle.
Let them give thanks to the LORD for His unfailing love
and His wonderful deeds for men,
for he satisfies the thirsty
and fills the hungry with good things.
PSALM 107:7-9

Prepare Your Heart

D o your prayers make any difference? The following story was reported by a missionary at his home church.

While serving at a small field hospital in Africa, I traveled every two weeks through the jungle to a nearby city for supplies. This requires camping overnight halfway. On one of these trips, I saw two men fighting in the city. One was seriously hurt, so I treated him and witnessed to him about the Lord Jesus Christ. I then returned home without incident. Upon arriving in the city several weeks later, I was approached by the man I had treated earlier. He told me he had known that I carried money and medicine. He said, "Some friends and I followed you into the jungle knowing you would camp overnight. We waited for you to go asleep and planned to kill you and take your money and drugs. Just as we were about to move into your campsite, we saw that you were surrounded by 26 armed guards." I laughed at this and said, "I was certainly all alone out in the jungle campsite." The young man pressed the point, "No sir, I was not the only one to see the guards. My five friends also saw them, and we all counted them. It was because of those guards that we were afraid and left you alone." At this point of the church presentation in Michigan, one of the men in the church stood up and interrupted the missionary. He asked, "Can you tell me the exact date when this happened?" The missionary thought for a while and recalled the date. The man in the congregation then gave his side of the story. He stated, "On that night in Africa it was day here. I was preparing to play golf. As I put my bags in the car, I felt the Lord leading me to pray for you. In fact, the urging was so great that I called men of this church together to pray for you. Will all of those men who met to pray please stand?" The men who had met that day to pray together stood—there were 26 of them![1]

God hears and answers your prayers! The power in prayer is the power of your God who is the Creator of the universe. This is your final day of looking specifically at the prayer of the pilgrim. Once again, ask the Lord: "Lord, teach me to pray."

READ AND STUDY GOD'S WORD

Psalm 107 teaches much about the power of God and His deliverances as a result of our prayers.

1. Read Psalm 107 again and record what God did in answer to prayer. What was the pivotal action that brought about God's answer? Also record anything you learn about how God works in the lives of men and women and on earth.

2. Summarize in one sentence your most significant observation from Psalm 107 about how God answers prayer.

What is the greatest thing we can do for someone in trouble? What is the greatest action we can take in our own trials? And what is the greatest work we will ever do in life? Stand in the gap. What does it mean to stand in the gap? In 593 B.C., God called a man named Ezekiel as a prophet to the people of Israel. This was a dark time in the history of God's people. They were sinful and rebellious. Therefore, God had determined to send them into exile at the hands of the Babylonians. Ezekiel's ministry began before the siege of Jerusalem and extended to the exilic community in Babylon. For a nation in trouble, God revealed something that could make a difference.

3. Turn to Ezekiel 22. Read this chapter and record your observations and insights about:
   Israel's sins

What God intended to do as a result

What could have made a difference with God

4. To understand more clearly what it means to stand in the gap, turn to the examples of Moses and Samuel. Look up the following verses and record your observations. Take into account the context of each passage of Scripture.
   Psalm 106:16-23

   Exodus 32:7-14

   Deuteronomy 9:7–10:21

   1 Samuel 7:7-13

   1 Samuel 12:12-25

5. What do you think it means to stand in the gap? What difference do you think it makes to stand in the gap? (Two excellent reference tools that explain this biblical concept are *The Bible Knowledge Commentary* and *The Expositor's Bible Commentary*.[2])

6. *Optional:* Finally, consider this: what do your prayers accomplish? Look at the following verses and record your insights:

    Luke 22:31-32

    2 Corinthians 1:9-11

    1 Timothy 4:4-9

    James 5:13-18

    Isaiah 30:18-21

ADORE GOD IN PRAYER

What are the greatest needs in your life? Perhaps you have already written these needs on your Prayer Pages. What are the needs of those you love, family and friends? Will you stand in the gap and intercede for each of those needs? Then, as you stand, watch the mighty power of God in answer to your prayers!

YIELD YOURSELF TO GOD

God's plan for our individual lives will not be all that it can be unless we pray. Prayer releases the power of God to accomplish the will of God in situations and in the lives of people. Prayer is the channel through which God's will is brought to earth. . . . Jesus taught His disciples to pray, "Thy will be done in earth, as it is in heaven." . . . There is a gap however, between what God wills in heaven and what is happening on earth. . . . As intercessors, we stand in that gap, linking heaven's plan and earth's circumstances. . . . As an intercessor stands in the gap, the flow of God's power continues through the gap and reaches the need. Now the need becomes a reflection of the power of God.[3]

    JENNIFER KENNEDY DEAN IN *THE PRAYING LIFE: LIVING BEYOND YOUR LIMITS*

Intercession is the act of standing in the gap between *the need* we see and *the provision* of God that we long to see. It can pertain to the need of a person, a church, a city, or a nation. Although the Father does not need us to complete His plan for the ages, He continues to call us to participate in its fulfillment. I am convinced He allows us to participate in His plan because He still wants an intimate relationship with us, and the primary way to facilitate that intimacy is through intercession.[4]

ALICE SMITH IN *BEYOND THE VEIL*

Prayer is certainly not persuading God to do what we want Him to do. It is not bending the will of a reluctant God to our will. It does not change His purpose, although it may release His power. "We must not conceive of prayer as overcoming God's reluctance," says Archbishop Trench, "but as laying hold of His highest willingness."

AN UNKNOWN CHRISTIAN IN *THE KNEELING CHRISTIAN*

Prayer does not fit us for the greater works; prayer is the greater work.[5]

OSWALD CHAMBERS IN *PRAYER: A HOLY OCCUPATION*

What do you believe it means to be a prayer warrior? Think about this question, the quotations you have read, and the Scripture you have studied today. Are you convinced of God's power to do the impossible and to intervene in the circumstances of life? Will you pay the price in time and energy to enter into this most holy occupation?

ENJOY HIS PRESENCE

To you, Heavenly Father, I commend my comrades and friends on every part of life's great battlefield. Let no defeat discourage them. Let no sudden temptation overcome them. Let no long-continued sorrow wear out their loyalty or discourage their faith.[6]

F. B. MEYER IN *DAILY PRAYERS*

REST IN HIS LOVE

"You do not have, because you do not ask God" (James 4:2).
   "The prayer of a righteous man is powerful and effective" (James 5:16).
   "I waited patiently for the LORD; he turned to me and heard my cry" (Psalm 40:1).

DEAR FRIEND,

As you have come to the end of your week of quiet times in Psalm 107, take some time for the next two days and review what you have learned. You may use this time to complete any quiet times, look at additional Scripture, draw near to your Lord in prayer, and consult any commentaries. As you review, record in the space provided:

Your most significant insight

Your favorite quote

Your favorite verse

In this psalm those who have been redeemed by the gracious interpositions of God are summoned to praise him for a love which endures through all our rebuffs and back-slidings. Note how this refrain breaks out in vv. 8, 15, 21, and 31. The psalmist passes before us a series of pictures, selected from the stories of human suffering which have been repeated in all ages of human history. Travelers who have lost their way, captives, sick men, storm-tossed sailors are presented in as many panels or pictures. The psalmist says that whatever our trouble, there is only one way out of it—to cry to God. This is never in vain. There is always the saving help of his right hand; and there is always, therefore, the obligation of praise.[1]

F. B. MEYER IN *DEVOTIONAL COMMENTARY*

the faith of the pilgrim

week
seven

PSALM 73

two ways of life

Surely God is good to Israel,
to those who are pure in heart.
But as for me, my feet had almost slipped;
I had nearly lost my foothold.
For I envied the arrogant
when I saw the prosperity of the wicked.

PSALM 73:1-3

Prepare Your Heart

Alan Redpath makes a profound statement at the beginning of his excellent book *The Making of a Man of God*: "The Bible never flatters its heroes. It tells us the truth about each one of them in order that against the background of human breakdown and failure we may magnify the grace of God and recognize that it is the delight of the Spirit of God to work upon the platform of human impossibilities."[1] In your life with God, you have probably already noticed situations arise that seem to challenge what you know to be true from the Word of God. These are what Redpath has called "human impossibilities." What are you to do when this happens? In fact, why does it happen?

There is a reason. Your life with God as His pilgrim is to be lived on a higher plane than is available to those who do not know God. Your pilgrimage takes you where no earthly person may travel: the high places of God. However, to get there you must walk in a new way—the way of faith. This way is, as Ruth Paxson has said so well, "life on the highest plane."

Do you desire to traverse your pilgrimage on the high places with God? Then you must learn how to walk by faith. This week you will study this most necessary quality of a pilgrim of God. And you will learn that it is one of the best secrets to the great adventure of knowing God.

As you begin your time with the Lord this week, stop for a moment and think about what you have learned thus far in your study of the pilgrimage of the heart. Review what is meant by pilgrimage. What does it mean to be a pilgrim of God? Then be still and turn your gaze to your Lord. Write out a prayer to Him, asking Him to open the eyes of your heart and teach you about His character and His ways this week.

READ AND STUDY GOD'S WORD

1. This week, as you learn about the faith of the pilgrim, you will study Psalm 73, written by Asaph. Who was Asaph and why was he important? Twelve psalms are attributed to him. He was the leader of worship during David's reign. As you prepare to enter into the experience of this psalmist in order to understand the nature of faith, turn to the following verses and record what you learn about Asaph:

1 Chronicles 6:31-42

1 Chronicles 16:1-7,37

2 Chronicles 29:30

Nehemiah 12:45-46

2. In Psalm 73, Asaph records his own very personal experience of faith. Read this psalm and record your first impressions of his experience.

3. As you begin to think about what it means to live by faith, it is important to understand that there are two ways of life: sight and faith. One focuses on the temporal and the other on the eternal. One produces ignorance and the other understanding. One way results in despair and the other in hope. The beauty of Psalm 73 is that in it Asaph

describes his experience of both ways and shares how he moved from one to the other. Read Psalm 73 again and record what you learn about both ways of life. What does Asaph see and understand in each way? Record your insights in the space provided.

The life of sight (verses 2-16)	The life of faith (verses 17-28)

4. These two ways of life are described in other places in the Bible. Look at the following verses and record what you learn about the life of sight and the life of faith:

Jeremiah 17:5-8

Habakkuk 3:16-19

John 10:10

2 Corinthians 4:16-18

2 Corinthians 5:7

5. Hebrews 11 has been called the Hall of Fame of Faith. Look at Hebrews 11:1-6 and record what you learn about faith.

6. Describe these two ways of life in your own words.

7. How do you see these two ways of life in the world today?

8. Which way of life best describes your life? Which way would you like to live?

ADORE GOD IN PRAYER

As you talk with God today, think about how these two ways of life influence your prayers. When you walk by faith, how will that make a difference in prayer? Spend some quiet time talking with God about what you have learned today. Ask Him to enable you to walk by faith, not by sight. You may want to use your Prayer Pages to record any new prayer requests and God's answers to your prayers.

Our Father, remove from us the sophistication of our age and the skepticism that has come, like frost, to blight our faith and to make it weak. Bring us back to a faith that makes men great and strong, a faith that enables us to love and to live, the faith by which alone we can walk with Thee. We pray for a return of that simple faith, that old-fashioned trust in God, that made strong and great the homes of our ancestors who built this good land and who in building left us our heritage. In the strong name of Jesus, our Lord, we make this prayer. Amen.[2]

PETER MARSHALL IN THE PRAYERS OF PETER MARSHALL

YIELD YOURSELF TO GOD

Bill Bright shares the following in his book *Believing God for the Impossible:*

> The Christian life is an exciting, joy-filled adventure! Never before have I felt this more strongly or experienced this truth more fully than today, after more than 30 years of walking with our Lord. Jesus promised the full and abundant life for all those who walk in faith and obedience. "I came that they might have life, and might have it more abundantly" (John 10:10). . . . "He who believes in Me, the works that I do shall he do also, and greater than these shall he do, because I go to the Father" (John 14:12). . . . "If you ask anything in My name, I will do it" (John 14:14). But most Christians do not live joyful and fruitful lives. Why? Because they have a *limited view of God.* I am convinced that no one can ever begin to live supernaturally and have the faith to believe God for impossible things, if he does not know what God is like, or if he harbors misunderstandings about God and His character. Would you like to live a joyful, abundant and fruitful life—every day filled with adventure? You can![3]

Charles Spurgeon defined faith as "the foot of the soul by which it can march along the road of the commandments." He goes on to say that "love can make the feet move more swiftly but faith *is* the foot which carries the soul. Faith is the oil enabling the wheels of holy devotion and of earnest piety to move well."[4]

A. W. Tozer said, "Faith is not in itself a meritorious act; the merit is in the One toward Whom it is directed. Faith is a redirecting of our sight, a getting out of the focus of our own vision and getting God into focus."[5]

As God's pilgrim, what do you look at and dwell on each day? Is your gaze filled with the temporal or the eternal? Do you walk by sight or by faith? Are you experiencing the abundant life promised by Jesus?

ENJOY HIS PRESENCE

Jesus, Lover of My Soul

Jesus, lover of my soul,
Let me to Thy bosom fly,
While the nearer waters roll,
While the tempest still is high.
Hide me, O my Savior, hide,
'Til the storm of life is past;
Safe into the haven guide,
O receive my soul at last.

Other refuge have I none,
Hangs my helpless soul on Thee;
Leave, O leave me not alone,
Still support and comfort me.
All my trust on Thee is stayed,
All my help from Thee I bring;
Cover my defenseless head
With the shadow of Thy wing.

Plenteous grace with Thee is found,
Grace to cover all my sin;
Let the healing streams abound,
Make and keep me pure within.
Thou of life the fountain art,
Freely let me take of Thee;
Spring Thou up within my heart,
Rise to all eternity. Amen.

CHARLES WESLEY

REST IN HIS LOVE

"Blessed is the man who trusts in the LORD, whose confidence is in him. He will be like a tree planted by the water that sends its roots out by the stream. It does not fear when heat comes; its leaves are always green. It has no worries in a year of drought and never fails to bear fruit" (Jeremiah 17:7-8).

the step of faith

When I tried to understand all this,
it was oppressive to me
till I entered the sanctuary of God;
then I understood their final destiny.
PSALM 73:16-17

Prepare Your Heart

One of the great pilgrims of faith was Hannah Whitall Smith, a nineteenth-century Quaker. She and her husband, Robert Pearsall Smith, conducted evangelistic meetings in Europe, and both demonstrated deep devotion to Christ. Hannah suffered many devastating blows in her life. Four of her seven children died young. Her husband had several nervous breakdowns and became involved with another woman. He grew bitter against God and wanted nothing to do with following Christ. Two of her daughters suffered breakdowns, and one married and later divorced Bertrand Russell, a renowned atheist. Yet what do you suppose are the titles of her best-known books? *The Christian's Secret of a Happy Life* and *The God of All Comfort*. What was her secret? She had learned what it means to take the first step of faith, then the next step, and finally, to walk by faith. Have you learned the pilgrim's secret to life on the highest plane? Draw near to God today and ask Him to open your eyes to the life of faith.

READ AND STUDY GOD'S WORD

As you continue your study in Psalm 73, think about what you learned yesterday. You saw in this psalm that there are two ways of life. Today you will begin to see more clearly how to choose the life of faith that will lead to life on the highest plane. It is the life of the pilgrim, a life where more and more you find your home in God until you reach your grand destination: heaven.

1. Read Psalm 73 again. This time, look for the one critical action of Asaph that made the difference in his understanding and actions. Record your insights.

This psalm raises some important questions: How is faith initiated? When does faith begin? What prompts us to take the step of faith? What is our responsibility? What will God do? And finally, what is faith? These are the questions you will think about today.

Faith in the New Testament is the Greek word *pistis*, which means a firm persuasion, conviction, and belief in that which is true and real.[1] *Wuest's Word Studies* says, "Faith apprehends as a real fact what is not revealed to the senses. It rests on that fact, acts upon it, and is upheld by it in the face of all that seems to contradict it. Faith is real seeing."[2] The facts that you rely on are found in the Bible. Deuteronomy 8:3 makes this clear: "Man does not live on bread alone but on every word that comes from the mouth of the LORD." And Isaiah says, "The grass withers and the flowers fall, but the word of our God stands forever" (Isaiah 40:8).

2. Many events in the Bible demonstrate the step of faith. Look at the following events and then record your insights related to any of the questions asked previously.

Mark 4:35–5:1

Luke 7:1-10

3. Turn to Hebrews 11:7-40. Read this great chapter on faith and record your insights about faith. What kinds of actions are considered to be "by faith"? As you look at each

example of faith, write down the action and the promise from God that you think prompted the action. As you list these actions and promises, you will discover the steps of faith that are possible when God gives you a promise from His Word.

Noah (verse 7)

Abraham (verses 8-10)

Sarah (verses 11-12)

All these (verses 13-16)

Abraham (verses 17-19)

Isaac (verse 20)

Jacob (verse 21)

Joseph (verse 22)

Moses (verses 23-29)

Rahab (verse 31)

All these (verses 32-40)

4. Finally, where does faith come from, and how do you have the power to live by faith? Record your insights related to these two important principles, found in two passages:
  Hebrews 12:1-2 (where faith comes from)

  Acts 1:8 (power to live this life of faith)

5. Now that you have been able to think more deeply about faith, how would you define it?

6. Who or what initiates your faith? What prompts you to take the step of faith?

7. What does God do to prompt faith?

8. Why might you consider the life of faith to be life on the highest plane?

ADORE GOD IN PRAYER

O Lord, I have heard a good word inviting me to look away to Thee and be satisfied. My heart longs to respond, but sin has clouded my vision till I see Thee but dimly. Be pleased to cleanse me in Thine own precious blood, and make me inwardly pure, so that I may with unveiled eyes gaze upon Thee all the days of my earthly pilgrimage. Then shall I be prepared to behold Thee in full splendor in the day when Thou shalt appear to be glorified in Thy saints and admired in all them that believe. Amen.[3]

A. W. TOZER IN *THE PURSUIT OF GOD*

YIELD YOURSELF TO GOD

God's Word is truer than anything I feel. God's Word is truer than anything I experience. God's Word is truer than any circumstance I will ever face. God's Word is truer than anything in the world. Why? Because heaven and earth will pass away before God's Word will pass away. This means that no matter how I feel or what I experience, I can choose dependence on the Word of God as the unchanging reality of my life. . . . There have been other times when I have felt afraid or lonely or depressed. During some of these periods my heart has literally ached in anguish over the circumstances of life, and in those moments I have been the most tempted to doubt the truth of God's Word. But they were the points at which I had to *choose with my will* to believe His Word. Thousands of times my prayers have begun *Lord, I feel . . . but, Lord, Your Word says* . . . And I've found that He does bring my emotions in line with His Word, in His own timing and in His way.[4]

NEY BAILEY IN *FAITH IS NOT A FEELING*

But now the question is how to bring oneself to be satisfied in God when there is no *feeling*. And I do not know what else to say, but that it must be by faith. . . . I confess that it does seem an odd sort of thing to do, to become satisfied by saying one is satisfied, when one is not. But is not just what faith is described to be, "calling those things which be not as though they were?" What else can we do? In my own case, I just determined I *would* be satisfied with God alone. I *gave up* seeking after any feeling of satisfaction. . . . I said "Lord, thou art enough for me, just Thyself, without any of Thy gifts or Thy blessings. I have Thee and I am content. I *will be* content. I *choose* to be content. I *am* content." I said this by faith. I still have to say it by faith often. I have to do so this very evening, for I am not very well and feel what I expect thou would call "low." But it makes no difference how I feel. He is just the same, and He *is* with me, and I *am* His, and I am satisfied.[5]

HANNAH WHITALL SMITH IN *THE SECRET LIFE OF HANNAH WHITALL SMITH*

Faith is a tremendously active principle which always puts Jesus Christ first—Lord, Thou hast said so and so, it looks mad, but I am going to venture on Thy word. To turn head faith into a personal possession is a fight always, not sometimes. God brings us into circumstances in order to educate our faith, because the nature of faith is to make its object real.[6]

OSWALD CHAMBERS IN MY UTMOST FOR HIS HIGHEST

ENJOY HIS PRESENCE

What is your most significant insight today? Thank God for showing you these truths related to faith, that most important quality in the lives of His pilgrims. Write a prayer in your Journal expressing what is on your heart as a result of your time with God today.

REST IN HIS LOVE

"And this is the victory that has overcome the world—our faith" (1 John 5:4, NASB).

the progress of faith

When my heart was grieved
and my spirit embittered,
I was senseless and ignorant;
I was a brute beast before you.
Yet I am always with you;
you hold me by my right hand.
You guide me with your counsel,
and afterward you will take me into glory.
PSALM 73:21-24

Prepare Your Heart

Hind's Feet on High Places is an allegory about a creature named Much-Afraid who is invited by the Chief Shepherd to leave the Valley of Humiliation and travel with Him to the High Places. Much-Afraid greatly desires to go on this journey but is so crippled and weak that it seems impossible. However, the Chief Shepherd promises to go with Much-Afraid on the journey. Not only that, He promises to give Much-Afraid "hind's feet" so that she can inhabit the High Places with him. Finally, He promises to give her a new name.

The Chief Shepherd gives her two companions as guides along the way, whose names are Sorrow and Suffering. Strange companions. And yet, they proved to be perfect for the journey. When Much-Afraid makes it to her destination, she receives her new name, Grace and Glory.

This allegory makes clear what every pilgrim of God must understand: the life of faith is not achieved in a one-time event. It grows and progresses and matures. This "progress" or upward climb occurs in ways that sometimes seem strange. Faith is tested, and in the process, it grows. We mature, becoming more like Christ. We move from faith to faith (see Romans 1:17, NASB). Today, as you draw near to God, ask Him to open your eyes to this life of faith. Meditate on the following words as a preparation of heart:

Joy and Peace in Believing

Sometimes a light surprises the Christian while he sings;
It is the Lord, who rises with healing in His wings;
When comforts are declining, He grants the soul again
A season of clear shining, to cheer it after rain.

In holy contemplation we sweetly then pursue
The theme of God's salvation, and find it ever new;
Set free from present sorrow, we cheerfully can say,
Let the unknown tomorrow bring with it what it may.

It can bring with it nothing but He will bear us through;
Who gives the lilies clothing will clothe His people too;
Beneath the spreading heavens no creature but is fed;
And He who feeds the ravens will give His children bread.

Though vine nor fig tree neither their wonted fruit shall bear,
Though all the field should wither nor flocks nor herds be there;
Yet God the same abiding, His praise shall tune my voice,
For while in Him confiding I cannot but rejoice.[1]

WILLIAM COWPER

READ AND STUDY GOD'S WORD

Your pilgrimage with God is a journey in which you live as an alien in a foreign land and find your home more and more in God until you reach your grand destination: heaven. How do you find your home more and more in God? By making the walk of faith more and more the habit of your life. Faith in God and His Word makes the unseen world visible to your spiritual eyes of faith. It is vital that you understand the nature of faith. It is meant to be tried and tested. The trial of your faith is what proves it to be genuine and what makes it strong.

   1. Look at the following verses and record what you learn about faith:
      Ephesians 2:4-10 (note the relationship between faith and works)

      Romans 1:17

1 Timothy 6:12

James 1:1-4

James 2:14-26 (note the relationship among faith and works and obedience)

1 Peter 1:3-9

2. One of the great examples of a man of faith is Abraham. Read Genesis 22:1-18 and record the progress of Abraham's faith. What did he learn about God as a result of the testing of his faith?

ADORE GOD IN PRAYER

Today, as you talk with God, think about what He has done in your life in the last few years. What has He been teaching you this year? How has your faith been tested? How have you progressed in walking by faith? What have you learned about God? Use a page in your Journal to write a prayer to God, expressing what is on your heart.

YIELD YOURSELF TO GOD

You find no difficulty in trusting the Lord with the management of the universe and all the outward creation, and can your case be any more complex or difficult than these, that you need to be anxious or troubled about his management of it. Away with such unworthy doubtings! Take your stand on the power and trustworthiness of your God, and see how quickly all difficulties will vanish before a steadfast determination to believe. Trust in the dark, trust in the light, trust at night, and trust in the morning, and you will find that the faith, which may begin by a mighty effort, will end sooner or later by becoming the easy and natural habit of the soul.

HANNAH WHITALL SMITH IN *THE CHRISTIAN'S SECRET OF A HAPPY LIFE*

God has frequently to knock the bottom board out of your experience if you are a saint in order to get you into contact with Himself. God wants you to understand that it is a life of *faith*, not a life of sentimental enjoyment of His blessings. Your earlier life of faith was narrow and intense, settled around a little sun-spot of experience that had as much of sense as of faith in it, full of light and sweetness; then God withdrew His conscious blessings in order to teach you to walk by faith.[2]

OSWALD CHAMBERS IN *MY UTMOST FOR HIS HIGHEST*

Let your faith, then, throw its arms around all God has told you, and in every dark hour remember that *though now for a season, if need be, you are in heaviness through manifold temptations*, it is only like going through a tunnel. The sun has not ceased shining because the traveler through the tunnel has ceased to see it; and the Sun of righteousness is still shining because the traveler through the tunnel has ceased to see it; and the Sun of righteousness is still shining, although you in your dark tunnel do not see Him. Be patient and trustful, and wait. This time of darkness is only permitted that "the trial of your faith, being much more precious than of gold that perisheth, though it be tried with fire, might be found unto praise and honor and glory at the appearing of Jesus Christ."

HANNAH WHITALL SMITH IN *THE CHRISTIAN'S SECRET OF A HAPPY LIFE*

ENJOY HIS PRESENCE

> Believe and trust; through stars and suns,
> Through life and death, through soul and sense,
> His wise, paternal purpose runs;
> The darkness of His Providence
> Is starlit with Divine intents.[3]

MRS. CHARLES COWMAN IN *STREAMS IN THE DESERT*

REST IN HIS LOVE

"The righteous will live by his faith" (Habakkuk 2:4).

the object of faith

Whom have I in heaven but you?
And earth has nothing I desire besides you.
My flesh and my heart may fail,
but God is the strength of my heart
and my portion forever.
PSALM 73:25-26

Prepare Your Heart

A well-known talk show host once remarked that his problem with Christ was that he had no faith. Is that really the problem with those who do not launch out on the promises of God and embrace Christ? No. Everyone has faith. Even the atheist has faith and exercises it. Every morning the atheist gets out of bed. He often inserts a key into the ignition of his car and turns the key. His faith acts on the belief that there is indeed an engine in the car and that the car will start and take him to his destination. Where did the atheist get his facts so that he could take his step of faith? Probably both from the previous experience of driving his car and from the last time he looked under the hood.

The issue is never the presence or quantity of faith. The issue is, *What is the object of your faith?* God will often test your faith in order to educate it, to enlarge your view of His ways and character. The more accurate your view of God, the greater will be your ability to walk by faith.

The atheist got his facts from experience and sight. Where will you get your facts so that you can rest your faith on a firm foundation? Your facts must come only from the Word of God. The sole authority for your belief is the Word of God. Everything else may change, but God's Word lasts forever. Your experience of walking by faith in God and His Word is your encouragement to put your trust, your faith, once again in God. This is why the people of Israel were constantly reminded to "remember how the LORD your God led you" (Deuteronomy 8:2). It is imperative that you, as God's pilgrim, know and understand God's Word! Then you will, more and more, know and understand God and His ways. Today draw near to God and ask Him to quiet you and speak to your heart.

READ AND STUDY GOD'S WORD

1. Turn to Psalm 73. Read through this psalm again. Once Asaph entered the sanctuary of God, describe everything he then understood to be true of God.

2. Take some time to understand the great value of God's Word in your life. Yours is an objective faith and is meant to be placed in God and His Word. Look at the following verses and record what you learn about God's Word. Remember, it is in His Word that you will learn about God and His ways.

Psalm 119:50,105

John 8:31-32

John 17:17

1 Corinthians 2:9-14

Ephesians 6:17

2 Timothy 3:16-17

Hebrews 4:12

2 Peter 1:4

2 Peter 1:20-21

What is your most significant insight about the Word of God?

3. *Optional:* God desires to educate your faith so that you will believe Him for impossible things. Jesus said, "I tell you the truth, if you have faith as small as a mustard seed, you can say to this mountain, 'Move from here to there' and it will move. Nothing will be impossible for you" (Matthew 17:20-21). One servant of God gained a gigantic view of God as a result of a great testing of faith. Job lost almost everything and came to the point of uttering one of the greatest cries of faith: "Though he slay me, yet will I hope in him" (Job 13:15). Turn to Job 38:1–40:5. In this passage God reveals Himself in a new way to Job. Record your most significant insights about God as you read what God says to him. Then read Job 42:10-16 and take note of the outcome of Job's trial.

ADORE GOD IN PRAYER

Meditate on what you learned today about the object of your faith: God and His Word. Turn to Job 38:31-41 and worship God for who He is as you think about how He described Himself to Job. Praise Him for each of His attributes and actions that you have seen in His Word. Make this a time of adoration of your great and awesome God.

Yield Yourself to God

A. W. Tozer introduces his book *The Knowledge of the Holy* with the following words:

> The Church has surrendered her once lofty concept of God and has substituted for it one so low, so ignoble, as to be utterly unworthy of thinking, worshiping men. This she has done not deliberately, but little by little and without her knowledge; and her very unawareness makes her situation all the more tragic. . . . The decline of the knowledge of the holy has brought on our troubles. A rediscovery of the majesty of God will go a long way toward curing them. . . . If we would bring back spiritual power to our lives, we must begin to think of God more nearly as He is.[1]

> Our view of God determines the quality of our faith. A small view of God results in a small faith. But great faith is the result of a correct biblical view of God as one who is great and worthy of our trust![2]
>
> BILL BRIGHT IN *BELIEVING GOD FOR THE IMPOSSIBLE*

> It is not a question of acquaintance with ourselves, or of knowing what we are, or what we do, or what we feel; it is simply and only a question of becoming acquainted with God, and getting to know what He is, and what He does, and what He feels. Comfort and peace can never come from anything we know about ourselves, but only and always from what we know about Him.
>
> HANNAH WHITALL SMITH IN *THE GOD OF ALL COMFORT*

How well do you know your God? Are you more focused on your circumstances, on how you feel, or on the character of God?

Enjoy His Presence

How Firm a Foundation

How firm a foundation, ye saints of the Lord,
Is laid for your faith in His excellent Word!
What more can He say than to you He hath said,
To you who for refuge to Jesus have fled?

Fear not, I am with thee; O be not dismayed,
For I am thy God, and will still give thee aid.
I'll strengthen thee, help thee, and cause thee to stand,
Upheld by My righteous, omnipotent hand.

When through deep waters I call thee to go,
the rivers of woe shall not thee overflow;
for I will be with thee, thy troubles to bless,
and sanctify to thee thy deepest distress.

When through fiery trials thy pathway shall lie,
My grace, all sufficient, shall be thy supply.
The flame shall not hurt thee; I only design
Thy dross to consume and thy gold to refine.

"K" IN RIPPON'S *A Selection of Hymns*

REST IN HIS LOVE

"Let us fix our eyes on Jesus, the author and perfecter of our faith" (Hebrews 12:2).

the result of faith

Those who are far from you will perish;
  you destroy all who are unfaithful to you.
  But as for me, it is good to be near God.
I have made the Sovereign LORD my refuge;
  I will tell of all your deeds.
PSALM 73:27-28

Prepare Your Heart

At the beginning of this week you read Alan Redpath's statement that "the Bible never flatters its heroes." The Bible is filled with ordinary people whose lives became the platform to display a magnificent, majestic, awesome, extraordinary God. While they made great mistakes and failed at times, God dwelt in their midst and imparted a supernatural life to them. He gave them the promise of eternal life, and they endured the suffering of the present with the hope of an unseen future.

What is the result of your life of faith? Is it really worth it all? God's Word says, "No eye has seen, no ear has heard, no mind has conceived what God has prepared for those who love him" (1 Corinthians 2:9). The big result of faith is summed up in one word: *sight*. Your faith becomes sight both in this world and in the life to come. You see God at work now in amazing and supernatural ways at times. And when you step from this world to your new life in eternity, the facade of this world will simply melt away to reveal the truth of the unseen kingdom of God. Then you will know. Then you will truly see. And then you will be able to say, more than you can say today, that it was truly worth it all.

Jesus said, "Blessed are those who have not seen and yet have believed" (John 20:29). Oh, how blessed and precious you are to your Lord! Ask God today to open your eyes that you might behold wonderful things from His Word. And thank Him for His unseen, yet nevertheless very real, presence in your life.

READ AND STUDY GOD'S WORD

1. In Psalm 73:27-28, Asaph expressed the experience of a life lived by faith. Read these verses and record your insights. What do you notice about his declarations? What is he saying? Describe his experience with God.

2. How does Peter describe the life of faith and the great result in 1 Peter 1:8-9?

3. The result of our faith is that it shall become sight. What will we see in this life and in eternity? How does God fulfill His Word? Record your insights as you meditate on the following promises from God's Word:

Jeremiah 17:7-8

Matthew 6:31-33

Romans 8:28-29

1 Corinthians 2:9-10

2 Corinthians 2:14

Philippians 2:13

Philippians 4:19

1 John 3:2

Revelation 22:4-5

4. Describe what it means to you that your faith will become sight.

Adore God in Prayer

This week you have been thinking about the faith of the pilgrim. You have probably thought about your own life and evaluated your steps of faith. Always remember that even when we are faithless, He remains faithful (see 2 Timothy 2:13). Do not be discouraged if your steps of faith seem small compared to what you have seen in God's Word. You are not alone. Every pilgrim is on the pilgrimage of faith, and God is educating each one as to who He is and what He can and will do in his or her life. So,

> let us throw off everything that hinders and the sin that so easily entangles, and let us run with perseverance the race marked out for us. Let us fix our eyes on Jesus, the author and perfecter of our faith, who for the joy set before him endured the cross, scorning its shame, and sat down at the right hand of the throne of God. Consider him who endured such opposition from sinful men, so that you will not grow weary and lose heart. (Hebrews 12:1-2)

Come before the Lord now in the stillness of this moment and lay at His feet everything that would keep you from walking by faith in His Word. Ask Him, as the author and perfecter of faith, to strengthen you so that your faith will not fail (just as Jesus prayed for Peter in Luke 22:32). And then, ask God to enable you to run with perseverance the race marked out for you. Ask Him to enable you to enter into the great adventure of knowing Him.

Declare with God in a statement of faith, as Asaph did, that indeed it is good to be near God and that He is the strength of your heart and your portion forever!

YIELD YOURSELF TO GOD

It may sometimes seem so impossible that the Lord can or does save that the words will not say themselves inside, but have to be said aloud, forcing one's lips to utter them over and over, shutting one's eyes and closing one's ears against every suggestion of doubt no matter how plausible it may seem. These declarations of faith often seem untrue at first, so apparently real are the seen reasons for doubt and discouragement. But the unseen facts are truer than the seen, and if the faith that lays hold of them is steadfastly persisted in, they never fail in the end to prove themselves to be the very truth of God. According to our faith it always must be unto us, sooner or later, and when we shout the shout of faith, the Lord invariably gives the victory of faith.

HANNAH WHITALL SMITH IN *THE GOD OF ALL COMFORT*

ENJOY HIS PRESENCE

By day and by night, in life and in death, may I ever be true to you, O Lover of my soul, my ceaseless Friend, my unchangeable Savior. Into your hands I commit my soul.[1]

F. B. MEYER IN *DAILY PRAYERS*

REST IN HIS LOVE

"Though you have not seen him, you love him; and even though you do not see him now, you believe in him and are filled with an inexpressible and glorious joy, for you are receiving the goal of your faith, the salvation of your souls" (1 Peter 1:8-9).

DEAR FRIEND,

These two days are your opportunity to spend time meditating on the truths you have learned about the faith of the pilgrim. You may use these days to review your quiet times and complete any unfinished studies. You may also choose to spend extra time alone in silence and solitude with your Lord. You may wish to listen to worship music or go for a walk with your Lord. You may also consult any commentaries on Psalm 73 and record your insights in your Journal. Also, record the following:

Your most significant insight

Your favorite quote

Your favorite verse

God is my portion forever—In spite of all the follies and sins of the past and present we may have God's constant presence; and in Him we can have all and more than all that the godless find in their wealth. God in heaven; God in the pathway of daily life; God in the heart—this is blessedness.[1]

F. B. MEYER IN *CHOICE NOTES ON THE PSALMS*

the home of the pilgrim

week
eight

PSALM 27

you are everything i need, Lord

The LORD is my light and my salvation —
whom shall I fear?
The LORD is the stronghold of my life —
of whom shall I be afraid?

PSALM 27:1

Prepare Your Heart

It is difficult to believe that this study is nearing the end. You are to be commended for spending time with God in His Word to grow in your relationship with Him. You have been focusing on this incredible perspective of pilgrimage that is found throughout God's Word. You have learned that you are on a pilgrimage of the heart. To be on pilgrimage means that you are increasingly finding your home in God while you live your life on earth as one who journeys in a foreign land until you reach your grand destination: heaven.

Standing behind this great and wonderful truth of pilgrimage is an implied truth that you must see as you close your studies in the Psalms. That is, there is a vast kingdom to which you belong that encompasses a place, a relationship, and a world that is eternal, unchanging, and permanent: the kingdom of God. Your pilgrimage would hold no meaning without the existence of God and His kingdom.

The Bible teaches that God has chosen a people to be His own, to be a part of His kingdom that exists under His rule, and to have the hope of living in His kingdom forever. It is important to state that the life of pilgrimage is the life lived with God. And one who lives with God is a true pilgrim indeed.

The pilgrim of God acts differently from one who is in the world. He or she has different priorities, affections, and attachments. The pilgrim evaluates events in a different way from the world. Quantity is not as important as quality. Obscurity is not a failure, and poverty is not a liability. The greatest Friend of the pilgrim is the One who cannot be seen yet is ever present and who leads every step of the way: the Lord Jesus Christ. And when the pilgrim steps from time into eternity, he or she will be met by this One who has led. Face to face, the pilgrim will have the great pleasure of hearing those wonderful words: "Well done, good and faithful servant!" (Matthew 25:21).

How can you live as God's pilgrim on the pilgrimage of the heart? Our last week of study is going to focus on the words of the one who was called by God "a man after my own heart" (Acts 13:22). When David was in danger of losing his life before God fulfilled His promise to make him king, he wrote Psalm 27. These words reveal the true heart of a pilgrim, and they demonstrate the commitment of a pilgrim. The real question we must ask as we close our studies is this: How can we find our home more and more in God and live as aliens in a foreign land? In David's pilgrim heart you will see some of the secrets.

As you begin this week with the Lord, ask Him to give you a pilgrim's heart with a single eye and single purpose, that you might run your race with endurance until you see Him face to face. Take a few moments to think about your own pilgrimage. Are you finding your home more and more in God? Do you have the heart of a pilgrim?

READ AND STUDY GOD'S WORD

Psalm 27 is one of the greatest psalms David ever wrote. He wrote it during a time of great danger; probably when Saul threatened his life. This was one of the great trials of David's life and challenged what he knew to be true about God. In his words, you will understand more clearly what it really means to be a pilgrim on pilgrimage.

1. It is thought that the events of 1 Samuel 23 are the background for Psalms 27, 31, and 54. Read 1 Samuel 23 and describe the events that brought about the writing of these psalms.

2. Read Psalm 27 as a journal entry from David during this time in his life. What is your impression of David and his heart for the Lord?

3. The first clue into David's heart and his life with God is the most repeated word in the psalm: *Lord*. Read Psalm 27 again, and circle or underline every occurrence of *Lord*, or pronouns referring to the Lord. Then record everything you learn about the Lord in Psalm 27.

The Hebrew word translated "LORD" is *Yahweh* (also known as *Jehovah*) and is the name of God most frequently used in the Old Testament, occurring approximately 5,320 times.[1] What is the significance of this name? Keep in mind that every time God gives His name to His people, it is with the purpose of revealing Himself—His ways and character. If He did not give His name to His people, they could not know Him, for He cannot be known except through His own revelation. He first revealed Himself as *Yahweh* in Genesis 2:4 in combination with the name *Elohim*. In *Elohim* God revealed Himself in greatness and glory as the Creator of the universe. In *Yahweh* God revealed Himself as the One who will always be. He is personal, self-existent, and absolute. In this name, God's people began to understand that God was unchanging and ever present. In his *Synonyms of the Old Testament*, Robert Baker Girdlestone says, "God's personal existence, the continuity of His dealings with man, the unchangeableness of His promises, and the whole revelation of His redeeming mercy gather round the name *Jehovah (Yahweh)*."[2] To the people of Israel, the name *Yahweh* was associated with righteousness and holiness and was so sacred that they were afraid to even pronounce it. Therefore, they substitute (even to this day) either *Adonai* or "the Name" when speaking it out loud.[3]

4. With that in mind, look at the following occurrences of *Yahweh* and record what you learn about Him: both His character and ways as *Yahweh*. *Yahweh* is translated "LORD" (in small capital letters).

Genesis 15:1

Exodus 3:1-15 ("I AM WHO I AM" is YHWH, rendered "LORD" in English translations of the Old Testament)

Exodus 14:13-14; 15:3

Exodus 19:23–20:22

Joshua 1:8-9

Isaiah 43:10-11

Isaiah 52:9-10

Isaiah 53:1-6

Summarize in one sentence your favorite insight about *Yahweh* in these verses. Keep in mind there is so much more for you to learn about your LORD—it will take eternity!

5. What do you think is the significance of the repetition of LORD by David throughout Psalm 27?

6. How well did David know God, and who did David know God to be, if he knew Him as *Yahweh?*

7. What do you see about David's heart for the Lord and his life commitment?

8. Describe what you have seen about the "home" of the pilgrim. Where is it that the pilgrim dwells according to Psalm 27? How does one make his or her home in God?

ADORE GOD IN PRAYER

David exhibits an exclusive commitment to His Lord in Psalm 27. There is no other One for him. It is the Lord who is his light, salvation, and strength. As you have studied what it means to be on pilgrimage these eight weeks and have seen David's heart today, what is your commitment to the Lord? Is He everything to you in life? Is He your priority? Write a prayer in your Journal, expressing all that is on your heart.

YIELD YOURSELF TO GOD

Our dwelling place is the place where we live, and not the place we merely visit. It is our home. All the interests of our earthly lives are bound up in our home; and we do all we can to make them attractive and comfortable. But our souls need a comfortable dwelling place even more than our bodies. . . . It is of vital importance, then, that we should find out definitely where our souls are living. The Lord declares that he has been our dwelling place in all generations, but the question is, Are we living in our dwelling place? . . . The truth is, our souls are made for God. He is our natural home, and we can never be at rest anywhere else.

Hannah Whitall Smith in The God of All Comfort

Alan Redpath comments on Psalm 27 in *The Making of a Man of God:*

The great theme of this Psalm, the burden on David's heart, is his longing for an intimate fellowship with the LORD and a constant light upon his path. He desired to live so close that when he heard just a whisper from God to his heart, saying "seek ye my face," immediately his heart would answer, "Thy face, Lord, will I seek" (27:8). He was learning something that only adversity can teach any of us; that is, to calm his fears, to steady his life, to stand still and watch for the salvation of God, to wait for a clear word of direction.[4]

Have you made your home in God? Have you discovered when the skies darken and the clouds roll in that the Lord is your light, your salvation, your strength, and everything you need?

Enjoy His Presence

What is your most significant insight today from your quiet time with God? How can you apply it to your life today?

Rest in His Love

"I command you—be strong and courageous! Do not be afraid or discouraged. For the LORD your God is with you wherever you go" (Joshua 1:9, NLT).

i seek one thing

One thing I ask of the LORD,
this is what I seek:
that I may dwell in the house of the LORD
all the days of my life,
to gaze upon the beauty of the LORD
and to seek him in his temple.
PSALM 27:4

Prepare Your Heart

Who has influenced your relationship with Christ? What people have been examples to you in your walk with the Lord? Corrie ten Boom survived Ravensbruck and was a strong witness for Jesus Christ in spite of the horrors and cruelty of a concentration camp. Hannah Whitall Smith had a husband who gave up his commitment to the Lord and a daughter who married an atheist. Yet she wrote *The Christian's Secret of a Happy Life* and *The God of All Comfort.* Jim Elliot said, "He is no fool who gives what he cannot keep to gain what he cannot lose," and was martyred by the Auca Indians in the jungles of Ecuador.

What do we love about those who have greatly influenced us? They ran their race well. They finished their course. They ran to win. They were pilgrims who fixed their eyes on their goal. They were always reaching for the prize. Nowhere is this more evident than in the words of David in the midst of his great trials. He said, "One thing I have asked of the LORD." One thing! And what was his goal? Intimacy with God. He wanted to "dwell in the house of the LORD all the days" of his life, "to gaze upon the beauty of the LORD." Everything David did revolved around his life goal. In the difficult times, he kept his eyes focused on his goal.

David was a relational thinker instead of a terminal thinker. This is the next quality of a pilgrim's heart. Relational thinking is "the process of relating activities and knowledge to an objective. Terminal thinking is defined as the process whereby activity and knowledge are

227

objective and ends within themselves."[1] The pilgrim has the heart of a winner with one objective and is single-minded in reaching that goal. This is another secret to finding your home more and more in God and less and less in this temporal world.

Do you know your overall goal in life? Is that goal determined by what God has shown you in His Word? From your life goal will flow your life message and ministry. Ask God to help you know your goal and then help you become a relational thinker so that your steps in your pilgrimage might move you closer to your goal.

READ AND STUDY GOD'S WORD

1. Turn to Psalm 27:4. Here you see David's heart more clearly. Write out Psalm 27:4 word for word.

2. How would you describe David's goal? What was the "one thing" he desired?

3. David had learned to relate everything to his goal. Look at the following events and describe how David's actions reveal a heart fixed on the goal of intimacy with God:
    1 Samuel 24:1-7

    2 Samuel 2:1-2

    2 Samuel 6:12-23

2 Samuel 7:18-22

1 Chronicles 16:1-7

4. *Optional:* God's pilgrims have hearts fixed on the goal given to them by God. This is clear in the Bible and is a vital part of finding your home in God. Look at the following examples and record what you learn about having a goal and relating everything in life to that goal. (If you are short on time, choose one verse from the Old Testament, one from the example of Jesus, and one from the example of Paul. You can always return to the other Scriptures at another time). Think about how you can follow David's example of relating everything to his goal of intimacy of God.

What God Has Said in the Old Testament
Jeremiah 9:23-24

Micah 6:8

The Example of Jesus
Matthew 6:33

Luke 5:31-32

Luke 9:51

John 4:34

The Example of Paul
1 Corinthians 9:22-27

Philippians 3:7-14

5. Summarize what you have seen about the "one thing" in life. What is most important in life for a pilgrim of God?

ADORE GOD IN PRAYER
Ask God today to begin forming His life goal for you in your heart. Ask Him to give you a verse that will guide you through life. You may want to write these requests on your Prayer Pages. Then, when God answers, you can record the date and the way He answered you.

> Lord, as I come to You with tears
> For all the wasted days and years
> And lay here humbly at Your feet,
> My precious One, my Refuge sweet,
> Asking that You take control and
> Let me have one thought, one goal:
> To follow You with all my heart
> Whatever path You may impart,
> That those who may be looking on
> Won't see this weak and useless one,
> But only see my Savior bright,
> His glory as my strength, my light.[2]

DEBRA COLLINS, WRITTEN AS A RESULT OF STUDYING *PILGRIMAGE OF THE HEART*

YIELD YOURSELF TO GOD

What verses have been most significant to you since you have known the Lord? Write them out, word for word, in your Journal. Is there a similar theme in all the verses that seems to be what God has been teaching you? Ask God to define His goals for you.

From your study of God's Word thus far, can you write out a goal based on what you have learned from the Lord in His Word? Is there a particular verse(s) that is significant from which this goal may be derived? For example, if Psalm 27:4 stands out to you, then you might say your goal in life is to know God and grow in intimacy with Him. Your goals should always be based on what you discover in God's Word. As you walk with the Lord and He teaches you more and more, your goal may change. Use the space provided to record your ongoing thoughts in the next year about a life verse and a life goal.

My life verse (the most significant verse or verses that God has shown you)

My life goal (restate this goal in the days and years to come)

One thing have I desired, my God, of Thee,
That will I seek, Thine house be home to me.
I would not breathe an alien, other air,
I would be with Thee, O Thou fairest Fair.
For I would see the beauty of my Lord,
And hear Him speak, Who is my heart's Adored.
O Love of loves, and can such wonder dwell
In Thy great Name of names, Immanuel?
Thou with Thy child, Thy child at home with Thee,
O Lord my God, I love, I worship Thee.[3]

AMY CARMICHAEL IN *TOWARD JERUSALEM*

ENJOY HIS PRESENCE

Robert Coleman says this of Jesus: "His life was ordered by His objective. Everything He did and said was part of the whole pattern. It had significance because it contributed to the ultimate purpose of His life in redeeming the world for God. This was the motivating vision governing His behavior. His steps were ordered by it. Mark it well. Not for one moment did Jesus lose sight of His goal."[4] In what ways can you order your steps today according to the objectives God has laid out for you? How do these goals change your priorities and actions? Record your thoughts in your Journal. As you walk with God, allowing Him to lead and guide you, you will see more and more that your life is a supernatural work of God.

REST IN HIS LOVE

"Do you not know that those who run in a race all run, but only one receives the prize? Run in such a way that you may win" (1 Corinthians 9:24, NASB).

yes, Lord

Teach me your way, O Lord;
lead me in a straight path because of my oppressors.
Psalm 27:11

Prepare Your Heart

What would cause a young woman to leave her family, her home, her friends, and the possibility of a husband to travel thousands of miles to a remote land to engage in an obscure work with no earthly gain or profit? Only the call to discipleship from one Person—Jesus Christ—could command such a life. And only the heart of a pilgrim could answer such a call from One greater than all earthly powers.

Such was the life of Amy Carmichael, who left home in Ireland at the age of twenty-six for missionary service in India for about fifty-six years. She suffered an accident while in India and was an invalid for the last twenty years before her death in 1951. She founded Dohnavur Fellowship, a Christian community in India, which became the haven for abandoned children and young girls who were rescued from Hindu temple prostitution. She wrote numerous books, including *If, Thou Givest . . . They Gather; Edges of His Ways; Gold by Moonlight; Toward Jerusalem;* and *Candles in the Dark.*

Amy Carmichael saw herself as a disciple of Jesus Christ, and He was her first love. In the biography *A Chance to Die,* Elisabeth Elliot describes her this way: "Her great longing was to have a 'single eye' for the glory of God. Whatever might blur the vision God had given her of His work, whatever could distract or deceive or tempt others to seek anything but the Lord Jesus Himself, she tried to eliminate. Why waste precious time, painful effort, on lesser things?"[1] Elliot introduces her biography of Carmichael with a challenge: "How shall we, accustomed to popular seminars on rights and how to feel comfortable, receive and transmit a faith that prized what the world despises (the Cross) and despised what the world prizes (all that dims the Cross)? The Christian life comes down to two simple things: trust and obedience."[2]

233

Two thousand years ago Jesus walked along the shores of the Sea of Galilee and issued a call to discipleship. Today He calls you to be His disciple. How will you answer the Lord's call to "follow Me, and I will make you fishers of men" (Matthew 4:19, NASB)? To say "Yes, Lord" is another great secret to finding your home more and more in God as you live life here on earth as an alien in a foreign land. As you begin your time with the Lord today, meditate on these words from Amy Carmichael.

> From prayer that asks that I may be
> Sheltered from winds that beat on Thee,
> From fearing when I should aspire,
> From faltering when I should climb higher,
> From silken self, O Captain, free
> Thy soldier who would follow Thee.
> From subtle love of softening things,
> From easy choices, weakenings,
> Not thus are spirits fortified,
> Not this way went the Crucified,
> From all that dims Thy Calvary,
> O Lamb of God, deliver me.
> Give me the love that leads the way,
> The faith that nothing can dismay,
> The hope no disappointments tire,
> The passion that will burn like fire,
> Let me not sink to be a clod:
> Make me Thy fuel, Flame of God.[3]

READ AND STUDY GOD'S WORD

1. David, the man after God's own heart, had the pilgrim heart of a disciple. He was a learner of his Lord. He desired to know God's ways and followed wherever He led. It was David's habit always to inquire of the Lord to know His character and ways. Turn to Psalm 27 and read the words again. Describe how David answered the call from God to follow Him.

2. What does it mean to be a disciple of Jesus Christ? Look at the following passages in the New Testament and record what you learn about disciples and discipleship:
   Matthew 7:24-27

Matthew 10:24-42

Matthew 19:27-30

Matthew 28:18-20

Luke 14:25-35

John 15:12-17

Acts 1:6-8

Romans 12:1-2

2 Timothy 2:1-10 (Paul's words to Timothy, his disciple)

Hebrews 13:7

3. *Optional:* How did others respond to the Lord's call to discipleship two thousand years ago? What do you learn from the following events about responding to the Lord's call to follow Him? (If you are short on time, choose one event and record your insights.)
    Matthew 4:18-22

Matthew 9:9

John 21:15-17

Luke 10:38-42

Acts 9:1-31 (Notice not only Paul's response to the call of Jesus, but also how Barnabas discipled Paul.)

Romans 1:1,14-17; 15:15-33; 1 Corinthians 9:23 (Note Paul's understanding of his call from the Lord Jesus Christ and how he followed Christ.)

4. A disciple is one who has made the decision to follow Christ, who has said "Yes, Lord," and who is personally and passionately attached to the Lord Jesus Christ. The disciple of Jesus Christ pours his or her life into others in such a way that they will become personally and passionately attached to Him. Are you a disciple of Jesus Christ? What is your most significant insight about discipleship from your time in God's Word today? How will you respond to the Lord's call to follow Him?

ADORE GOD IN PRAYER

Lord, I give up all my own plans and purposes, all my own desires and hopes, and accept Thy will for my life. I give myself, my time, my all utterly to Thee to be Thine forever. Fill me and seal me with Thy Holy Spirit. Use me as Thou wilt, send me where Thou wilt, work out Thy whole will in my life at any cost, now and forever.[4]

BETTY SCOTT STAM IN *YES* BY ANN KIEMEL ANDERSON

YIELD YOURSELF TO GOD

"Follow Me," said Jesus to the fishermen of Bethsaida, "and I will make you fishers of men." These words (whose originality stamps them as a genuine saying of Jesus) show that the great Founder of the faith desired not only to have disciples, but to have about Him men whom He might train to make disciples of others: to cast the net of divine truth into the sea of the world, and to land on the shores of the divine kingdom a great multitude of believing souls.[5]

A. B. BRUCE IN *THE TRAINING OF THE TWELVE*

YES
to the Cross.
to obedience . . . honesty . . .
reality . . . earnest heart.
to joy and sorrow.
ease and difficulty.
success and failure.
to forgiving.
to saying things that edify.
YES
because Jesus is the divine Yes.
because He changes everything.
He is my highest Fulfillment.
He's made me whole . . .
takes the bad and turns it to good.
He is my Song . . .
my reason to live.
for to me, to live is Christ.[6]

ANN KIEMEL ANDERSON IN *YES*

Are you willing to count the cost, follow Jesus Christ, and become a fisher of men and women? Will you say no to self and the distractions of the world? Will you say yes to God and invest your life in the things that last forever: the Triune God, His Word, and lives that are changed for Jesus Christ?

ENJOY HIS PRESENCE

Take My Life, and Let It Be Consecrated

Take my life and let it be consecrated, Lord, to Thee;
Take my hands and let them move at the impulse of Thy love,
At the impulse of Thy love.
Take my feet and let them be swift and beautiful for Thee;
Take my voice and let me sing always, only, for my King,
Always, only for my King.
Take my lips and let them be filled with messages for Thee;
Take my silver and my gold, not a mite would I withhold,
Not a mite would I withhold.
Take my love, my God, I pour at Thy feet its treasure store;
Take myself and I will be ever, only, all for Thee,
Ever, only, all for Thee.

FRANCES R. HAVERGAL

i stand before Christ and the world. my heart shouts an affirmation:
Jesus, i am a humble, lowly servant woman.
take me . . . all of me.
add anything. take away anything.
at any cost. with any price.
make me Yours. completely . . . wholly.
may i not be remembered for
how i wear my hair
or the shape of my face
or the people i know
or the crowds i've addressed.
may i be known for loving You . . .
for carrying a dream . . .
for building bridges
to the hurt and broken and lost in the world.
make me what You would be if You lived
in Person where i do.
may everything accomplished through my simple
life bring honor and glory to You.
take my human failures and flaws,
and use them to remind these who know me
that only You are God,

and i will always just be ann.
amen.
amen.[7]

ANN KIEMEL ANDERSON IN YES

Take some time now to write a prayer of dedication to your Lord that says yes to Him. Ask Him to teach you His ways and lead you in His paths.

REST IN HIS LOVE
"Follow Me, and I will make you fishers of men" (Matthew 4:19, NASB).

i am still confident

I am still confident of this:
I will see the goodness of the LORD
in the land of the living.
PSALM 27:13

Prepare Your Heart

The heart of God's pilgrim is fixed on a place that is not of this world: the kingdom of God. What is this kingdom, and what does it mean to belong to God's kingdom? Understanding the place where you belong will help you to find your home more and more in God and less and less in this world. It will not be so strange to be an alien to the things of this world when your gaze is filled with a far greater kingdom, one that lasts forever. Knowledge of the kingdom of God and the assurance of your place there will fuel your hope in this life. That hope is the ability to wait with a smile for God to carry out His promises.

Hope is one of the great marks of a pilgrim of God. And it is, as God's Word says in Hebrews 6:19, the anchor for your soul. As a preparation of heart, read Psalm 145 and record below any insights about the kingdom of God.

READ AND STUDY GOD'S WORD

1. Read Psalm 27:13. What was David's confidence? Describe his confidence in your own words.

2. As pilgrims of God, we have David's confidence and hope: the assurance of a bright future with God, a future that is true life indeed, a life that lasts forever. When Jesus walked on earth, He spoke of a kingdom not of this world. It was a heavenly kingdom. He was concerned to make certain that those on earth knew of the existence and importance of this kingdom. Not only that, He also made it clear that the kingdom of God reigned supreme. What do you know about the kingdom of God? Look at the following verses and record your insights. (Choose two verses in each section if time does not permit you to look at all of them.)

The Words of Jesus

Matthew 6:33

Matthew 13:45-46

Matthew 24:14

Matthew 25:31-36

Luke 4:42-44; 9:11

Luke 9:60-62

Luke 17:20-21

The Words of Paul
Romans 14:17

Colossians 1:13

2 Timothy 4:18

The Words of John in Revelation
1:6

11:15

12:10-11

21:21-27

3. How important was the kingdom of God to Jesus?

4. In what way is the kingdom of God present, and in what way is it yet to come?

5. What is your most significant insight about the kingdom of God?

6. How does knowing about the kingdom of God help you to be a pilgrim in this world, finding your home in God and living life here as an alien in a foreign land? (See example of Abraham in Hebrews 11:8-10.)

ADORE GOD IN PRAYER

Today, as you talk with God, lay the burdens of your heart at His feet. Bring to Him any personal requests and the needs of your family and friends. You may wish to turn to your Prayer Pages and write new requests. Review previous prayer requests and record any answers or additional promises from God's Word that relate to your requests. Remember, you are a child of the King, and your citizenship is in heaven. Be bold in your entrance into the throne room of God because your entry has been gained by the blood of your Savior, Jesus Christ.

YIELD YOURSELF TO GOD

The kingdom where Jesus was both King and Lawgiver was not to be a kingdom of this world: it was not to be here or there in space, but within the heart of man; it was not to be the monopoly of any class or nation, but open to all possessed of the requisite spiritual endowments on *equal terms*. . . . The works which the twelve were privileged to see were worth seeing, and altogether worthy of the Messianic King. They served to demonstrate that the King and the kingdom were not only coming, but come.[1]

A. B. BRUCE IN *THE TRAINING OF THE TWELVE*

The true Christian life, when we live near to God, is the rough draft of the life of full communion above. We have seen the artist make with his pencil, or with his charcoal, a bare outline of his picture. It is nothing more, but still one could guess what the finished picture will be from the sketch before you. One acquainted with the artist could see upon the canvas all the splendor of color peeping through the dark lines of the pencil. . . . We have much of heaven here; at any rate, we have the Lamb who is the glory of the eternal city; we have the presence of him that sits upon the throne among us even now; we have if not the perfect holiness of heaven, yet a justification quite as complete as that of the glorified; we have the "white robes," for "the blood of the Lamb" has washed them even now; and if we have not yet the palm branches of the final victory, yet thanks be to God, we are led in triumph in every place, and even now *this is the victory that overcomes the world, even our faith.* Therefore—*I would begin the music here, and so my soul should rise; Oh, for some heavenly notes to bear my passions to the skies.*[2]

CHARLES SPURGEON IN "HEAVEN BELOW" FROM SPURGEON'S SERMONS

Every day and every hour of every day, not only in the Church but in the home, in the workshop, in the business, in the office, in the political arena, in public and in private, I am Christ's man, I am Christ's woman, and I must act, I must live, I must walk, I must so conduct myself, so transact my business, so think and so speak that the Divine stamp will be on me and will be felt and seen everywhere. I must live with this ever before me, I am risen with Christ, and by my life, my neighbors, my friends, my servants, my master, my acquaintances and relatives must see that my heart is set on things above.[3]

GYPSY SMITH IN AS JESUS PASSED BY

Does your life exhibit your citizenship in the kingdom of God?

ENJOY HIS PRESENCE

Paul encouraged the church at Philippi in the following way: "Finally, brethren, whatever is true, whatever is honorable, whatever is right, whatever is pure, whatever is lovely, whatever is of good repute, if there is any excellence and if anything worthy of praise, dwell on these things" (Philippians 4:8, NASB). What were your most significant insights today that fit into these parameters? Will you let your mind dwell on these things today?

REST IN HIS LOVE

"Therefore, prepare your minds for action; be self-controlled; set your hope fully on the grace to be given you when Jesus Christ is revealed" (1 Peter 1:13).

i will wait for the Lord

Wait for the LORD;
be strong and take heart
and wait for the LORD.
PSALM 27:14

Prepare Your Heart

In the first century, as now, athletic games were extremely popular. Athletes were revered. Athletic games were held in just about every major city: Corinth, Ephesus, Rome. They would be held in stadiums, with huge crowds attending to watch. The athletes would train all year for these athletic games. Races were run, and only one prize was given. The prize was relatively simple—a wreath made of oak, ivy, myrtle, olive leaves, or flowers. This wreath—called *stephanos* in Greek—was the victor's crown. And even though it was simple, all the athletes wanted it. Why? Because of what came with it: glory and honor. It represented the highest of honors, and the winner of it was revered. Everyone knew that the one with the *stephanos* had worked the hardest, trained diligently, was the most disciplined, and was the best.

God has a *stephanos* to hand out to you as well. As a runner in this race of life, you need to know what the rules are—what it takes to win the prize. God's measure is different from man's. In the world, the prize always goes to the most capable, the most successful, the best looking, the most aggressive, or the one with the most brilliance. In God's realm, this is what it takes to win your *stephanos*, your victory crown:

- Invest your life in the things that count for eternity: people and God's Word.
- Long for the appearing of your Lord, Jesus Christ.
- Persevere under trials, stand firm in the tests of your faith, endure every hardship.
- Be faithful to God in everything, even to the point of death.

How is it possible? How can you keep your eyes on the goal, the prize, the *stephanos*, the victory crown? How can you stay in the race and advance toward the prize? Just follow the lead of the One who has run ahead of you, the One who is faithful and true and has overcome every obstacle. He wore a crown of thorns so that one day He can hand you your victory crown. That crown will never fade away. It represents the highest of all rewards: righteousness and eternal life.

On this, your last day of study in this book, it is fitting to look at David's final words in Psalm 27. He said to "wait for the LORD; be strong and take heart and wait for the LORD." Why would you want to wait for the Lord? So that you can keep your eyes on Him and follow Him. So that you can become the person He wants you to be. So that you will carry out God's purposes. So that you can have the best. So that you may experience the abundant life. And finally, so that you may, one day, receive your victory crown, your *stephanos*. Draw near to the Lord now and ask Him to quiet your heart and speak to you from His Word.

READ AND STUDY GOD'S WORD

What kind of pilgrim is able to wait on the Lord? It is the one with the mature heart, who has been tried and tested, and has gained the ability to endure. It is the pilgrim who is a disciple of Jesus Christ with a reckless, radical abandonment to the will of God. It is the one who is more than a conqueror through Jesus Christ. This is the pilgrim who is able to stand strong. This pilgrim knows his or her own weakness and finds strength in only one place: the Lord. This pilgrim is courageous because the Lord is a great warrior. This pilgrim has learned to sing in the dark night of the soul, runs to the Lord as a strong and mighty refuge, and is devoted not to religion but to the person of Jesus Christ. This pilgrim knows the language of God, the high privilege of prayer. This pilgrim knows how to walk by faith rather than sight and apprehend what is not seen by the eye. This pilgrim is on the pilgrimage of the heart, finding his or her home more and more in God while journeying through life as an alien in a foreign land until the grand destination is reached: heaven. Today you have the opportunity to look at what it means to "wait on the LORD."

1. The word *wait* in the Hebrew is *qawah*. It means "to wait or to look for with eager expectation. Waiting involves the very essence of a person's being. . . . Those who wait in true faith are renewed in strength so that they can continue to serve the Lord while looking for His saving work. There will come a time when all that God has promised will be realized and fulfilled."[1] What do you learn from the following verses about waiting on the Lord?
   Psalm 25:3-5

   Psalm 37:1-7,34

Psalm 62:5-8

Psalm 119:74,81,114

Psalm 130:1-6

Isaiah 40:30-31

Jeremiah 6:16

John 15:1-5

John 16:33

1 Corinthians 15:58

Philippians 3:20

Titus 2:11-13

1 Peter 4:19

2. Describe what it means to wait on the Lord. When you wait on the Lord, what does that involve?

ADORE GOD IN PRAYER

Take this time now to talk with the Lord about what you have been learning from Him. Take what has been most significant to you and write a prayer to your Lord in the space below.

YIELD YOURSELF TO GOD

Have you learned to wait on the Lord, no matter what, to be strong and take heart? May our words echo the words of the young pastor from Zimbabwe who was martyred for his faith in Jesus Christ. The following note was found in his office after his martyrdom:

I'm part of the fellowship of the unashamed. I have the Holy Spirit power. The die has been cast. I have stepped over the line. The decision has been made—I'm a disciple of His. I won't look back, let up, slow down, back away, or be still. My past is redeemed, my present makes sense, my future is secure. I'm finished and done with low living, sight walking, smooth knees, colorless dreams, tamed visions, worldly talking, cheap giving, and dwarfed goals.

I no longer need preeminence, prosperity, position, promotions, plaudits, or popularity. I don't have to be right, first, tops, recognized, praised, regarded, or rewarded. I now live by faith, lean in His presence, walk by patience, am uplifted by prayer, and I labor with power.

My face is set, my gait is fast, my goal is heaven, my road is narrow, my way rough, my companions are few, my Guide reliable, my mission clear. I cannot be bought, compromised, detoured, lured away, turned back, deluded, or delayed. I will not flinch in the face of sacrifice, hesitate in the presence of the enemy, pander at the pool of popularity, or meander in the maze of mediocrity.

I won't give up, shut up, let up, until I have stayed up, stored up, prayed up, paid up, preached up for the cause of Christ. I am a disciple of Jesus. I must go till He comes, give till I drop, preach till all know, and work till He stops me. And, when He comes for His own, He will have no problem recognizing me . . . my banner will be clear![2]

As quoted by Brennan Manning in The Signature of Jesus

Can you say the same thing? "When He comes for His own, He will have no problem recognizing me . . . my banner will be clear!"

Enjoy His Presence

And so fellow pilgrims, my challenge to you is to

> *Lay aside every encumbrance*
> *Fix your eyes on Jesus*
> *Fight the fight*
> *Finish your course*
> *Keep the faith*

Then on that day when you stand before the Lord and look into the eyes of the One who you have loved all these years, He will place your *stephanos* on your head. You will hear Him say, "Well done, good and faithful servant!" (Matthew 25:21). This will be your greatest honor and glory. Then you will know . . .

It was worth it all!

Rest in His Love

"No eye has seen, no ear has heard, and no mind has imagined what God has prepared for those who love him" (1 Corinthians 2:9, NLT).

Dear Friend,

In these last days of your study, it is fitting to take some time to think about your own pilgrimage. You wrote a special letter to the Lord at the beginning of this study on the page at the end of the Introduction. Turn to that prayer now and read what you wrote to the Lord. In your Journal, write a prayer of thanksgiving to the Lord for how He has worked in your life.

The following are some questions for you to think about. There are verses following each question that you may wish to meditate on, and you may want to write your insights in the spaces provided. God bless you as you continue on your pilgrimage with the Lord.

Questions for Pilgrims

1. Is your time and energy given to laying up treasure in heaven? (See Matthew 6:19-21; Matthew 16:24-25; Ephesians 5:15-21; Colossians 4:5.)

2. Are you more concerned with the things of this world or the things of God? (See Matthew 6:33; 1 John 2:15-17.)

3. Is your life characterized by love? (See Ephesians 4:31-32; Matthew 5:43-48.)

4. Is any job too small in service of the King of kings? Is any job too large when accomplished in the strength of the Creator of the universe? (See Colossians 3:23-24.)

5. In your suffering, are you giving up, or do you hope in God? (See Romans 5:3-5; 2 Corinthians 4:16-17; Hebrews 6:19; James 1:2-4.)

6. Do you see yourself as God's ambassador in a foreign land, or do you feel that you have no purpose in life? (See 2 Corinthians 2:14-17; 2 Corinthians 5:20.)

7. Are you consumed with pleasing God or pleasing yourself? (See Ephesians 5:6-10.)

8. Is joy becoming your strength for the journey? (See Nehemiah 8:10; John 15:11.)

9. Are you cultivating a rich inner life, a spiritual life, learning God's language of prayer and worship? (See 1 Samuel 16:7; James 4:8; 2 Chronicles 15:4.)

10. Are you well acquainted with the map for your journey? Is the Bible your guide as you traverse the landscape of your pilgrimage, or are you walking blindly through life? (See 2 Timothy 3:16-17; Isaiah 55:8-11.)

11. Do you focus on God's perspective in your circumstance, or is the world's view filling the gaze of your heart? (See 2 Corinthians 4:17-18; 5:7.)

12. Are you keeping your eyes on the goal, the upward call of God in Christ Jesus, or are you content with the mediocrity and compromise of this world? Are you looking forward to getting home to eternal life in heaven, and are you living as a member of your heavenly kingdom in this temporal world? (See Isaiah 25:6-9; Revelation 22:3-4; Philippians 3:8-14; Hebrews 12:1-2.)

now that you have completed these quiet times

You have spent eight weeks consistently drawing near to God in quiet time with Him. That time alone with Him does not need to come to an end. What is the next step? To continue your pursuit of God, you might consider other books of quiet times in this series: *A Heart That Dances: Satisfy Your Desire for Intimacy with God* and *Revive My Heart!: Satisfy Your Thirst for Personal Spiritual Renewal.*

You might choose to meet with friends as you spend time with the Lord using these books of quiet times. Leader's guides, audiotapes, and videotapes are available to accompany each book. Apply practical ideas on how to have a quiet time, including choosing a Bible reading plan, setting aside a time and a place, using devotional books, and recording your insights in a quiet-time notebook or journal.

Quiet Time Ministries has many resources to encourage you in your quiet time with God, including the Quiet Time Notebook, *Enriching Your Quiet Time* magazine, audiotapes, and videotapes. These resources may be ordered online from Quiet Time Ministries at www.quiet-time.org. You may also call Quiet Time Ministries to order or request a catalog.

For more information, you may call or write to Quiet Time Ministries:

P.O. Box 14007
Palm Desert, California 92255
(800) 925-6458, (760) 772-2357
E-mail: catherine@quiettime.org
www.quiettime.org

Pour out your heart like water in the presence of the Lord.
LAMENTATIONS 2:19, NIV

Pour out your heart like water in the presence of the Lord.
LAMENTATIONS 2:19, NIV

Pour out your heart like water in the presence of the Lord.
LAMENTATIONS 2:19, NIV

Pour out your heart like water in the presence of the Lord.
LAMENTATIONS 2:19, NIV

_____

_____

_____

_____

_____

_____

_____

_____

_____

_____

_____

_____

_____

_____

_____

_____

_____

_____

Pour out your heart like water in the presence of the Lord.
LAMENTATIONS 2:19, NIV

_____

_____

_____

_____

_____

_____

_____

_____

_____

_____

_____

_____

_____

_____

_____

Pour out your heart like water in the presence of the Lord.
LAMENTATIONS 2:19, NIV

Pour out your heart like water in the presence of the Lord.
LAMENTATIONS 2:19, NIV

Pour out your heart like water in the presence of the Lord.
LAMENTATIONS 2:19, NIV

Pour out your heart like water in the presence of the Lord.
LAMENTATIONS 2:19, NIV

Do not be anxious about anything, but in everything, by prayer and petition, with thanksgiving, present your requests to God. And the peace of God, which transcends all understanding, will guard your hearts and your minds in Christ Jesus.
PHILIPPIANS 4:6-7, NIV

PRAYER FOR _____

DATE:

SCRIPTURE:

REQUEST:

ANSWER:

PRAYER FOR _____

DATE:

SCRIPTURE:

REQUEST:

ANSWER:

Do not be anxious about anything, but in everything, by prayer and petition, with thanksgiving, present your requests to God. And the peace of God, which transcends all understanding, will guard your hearts and your minds in Christ Jesus.
PHILIPPIANS 4:6-7, NIV

PRAYER FOR _____

DATE:

SCRIPTURE:

REQUEST:

ANSWER:

PRAYER FOR _____

DATE:

SCRIPTURE:

REQUEST:

ANSWER:

Do not be anxious about anything, but in everything, by prayer and petition, with thanksgiving, present your requests to God. And the peace of God, which transcends all understanding, will guard your hearts and your minds in Christ Jesus.
PHILIPPIANS 4:6-7, NIV

PRAYER FOR _____

DATE:

SCRIPTURE:

REQUEST:

ANSWER:

PRAYER FOR _____

DATE:

SCRIPTURE:

REQUEST:

ANSWER:

Do not be anxious about anything, but in everything, by prayer and petition, with thanksgiving, present your requests to God. And the peace of God, which transcends all understanding, will guard your hearts and your minds in Christ Jesus.
PHILIPPIANS 4:6-7, NIV

PRAYER FOR _____

DATE:

SCRIPTURE:

REQUEST:

ANSWER:

PRAYER FOR _____

DATE:

SCRIPTURE:

REQUEST:

ANSWER:

Do not be anxious about anything, but in everything, by prayer and petition, with thanksgiving, present your requests to God. And the peace of God, which transcends all understanding, will guard your hearts and your minds in Christ Jesus.
PHILIPPIANS 4:6-7, NIV

PRAYER FOR _____

DATE:

SCRIPTURE:

REQUEST:

ANSWER:

PRAYER FOR _____

DATE:

SCRIPTURE:

REQUEST:

ANSWER:

Do not be anxious about anything, but in everything, by prayer and petition, with thanksgiving, present your requests to God. And the peace of God, which transcends all understanding, will guard your hearts and your minds in Christ Jesus.

PHILIPPIANS 4:6-7, NIV

PRAYER FOR _____

DATE:

SCRIPTURE:

REQUEST:

ANSWER:

PRAYER FOR _____

DATE:

SCRIPTURE:

REQUEST:

ANSWER:

Do not be anxious about anything, but in everything, by prayer and petition, with thanksgiving, present your requests to God. And the peace of God, which transcends all understanding, will guard your hearts and your minds in Christ Jesus.
PHILIPPIANS 4:6-7, NIV

PRAYER FOR _____

DATE:

SCRIPTURE:

REQUEST:

ANSWER:

PRAYER FOR _____

DATE:

SCRIPTURE:

REQUEST:

ANSWER:

Do not be anxious about anything, but in everything, by prayer and petition, with thanksgiving, present your requests to God. And the peace of God, which transcends all understanding, will guard your hearts and your minds in Christ Jesus.
PHILIPPIANS 4:6-7, NIV

PRAYER FOR _____

DATE:

SCRIPTURE:

REQUEST:

ANSWER:

PRAYER FOR _____

DATE:

SCRIPTURE:

REQUEST:

ANSWER:

Do not be anxious about anything, but in everything, by prayer and petition, with thanksgiving, present your requests to God. And the peace of God, which transcends all understanding, will guard your hearts and your minds in Christ Jesus.
PHILIPPIANS 4:6-7, NIV

PRAYER FOR _____

DATE:

SCRIPTURE:

REQUEST:

ANSWER:

PRAYER FOR _____

DATE:

SCRIPTURE:

REQUEST:

ANSWER:

notes

INTRODUCTION

1. Henri Nouwen, "Moving from Solitude to Community to Ministry," *Leadership Journal*, vol. 15, no. 2 (Spring 1995), p. 81.

2. James Montgomery Boice, *Psalms*, vol. 1 (Grand Rapids, Mich.: Baker Book House Company, 1994), p. 9. Used by permission.

3. Martin Luther, *Psalms with Introductions by Martin Luther* (St. Louis, Mo.: Concordia, 1993), p. 3.

4. J. I. Packer, *Knowing God* (Downers Grove, Ill.: InterVarsity, 1973), p. 16. Used by permission.

WEEK 1, DAY 1

1. J. J. Stewart Perowne, *Commentary on the Psalms* (Grand Rapids, Mich.: Kregel Publications, 1989), p. 115.

2. James Montgomery Boice, *Psalms*, vol. 2 (Grand Rapids, Mich.: Baker Book House, 1996), pp. 687-693.

3. Brent Curtis and John Eldridge, *The Sacred Romance* (Nashville, Tenn.: Thomas Nelson Publishers, 1997), pp. 10, 144. Used by permission.

WEEK 1, DAY 2

1. From the book *The Pursuit of God* by A. W. Tozer. Copyright 1982, 1993 by Christian Publications, Inc., Camp Hill, Penn. Used with permission. Page 20.

2. From *The Pursuit of God*, pp. 66-67. Used with permission.

WEEK 1, DAY 3

1. Gordon S. Wakefield, ed., *The Westminster Dictionary of Christian Spirituality* (Philadelphia: The Westminster Press, 1983), p. 302. Used by permission.

2. John Bunyan, *Prayer* (Carlisle, Penn.: The Banner Of Truth Trust, 1662, 1995), p. 19.

3. *Man of Prayer*, Frank C. Laubach, 1990, New Readers Press, U.S. Publishing Division of Laubach Literacy, Syracuse, New York, used by permission. Page 52.

4. *The Complete Word Study Dictionary*, compiled and edited by Spiros Zodhiates, AMG Publishers, Chattanooga, Tenn., 1992. Page 937. Used by permission.

WEEK 1, DAY 4

1. Taken from *Linguistic Key to the Greek New Testament* by Fritz Rienecker and Cleon Rogers. Copyright © 1976 by The Zondervan Corporation. Used by permission of Zondervan Publishing House. Page 705.

2. J. D. Douglas, ed., *New Bible Dictionary* (Downers Grove, Ill.: InterVarsity, 1962), p. 119.
3. Dietrich Bonhoeffer, *Psalms: The Prayer Book of the Bible* (Minneapolis, Minn.: Augsburg, 1974), p. 15.
4. Taken from *The Green Letters* by Miles J. Stanford. Copyright © 1975 by Miles J. Stanford. Used by permission of Zondervan Publishing House. Page 14.
5. Kenneth S. Wuest, *Wuest's Word Studies of the Greek New Testament*, vol. 2 (Grand Rapids, Mich.: Eerdmans, 1973), p. 24.
6. Excerpted from *The Green Letters* by Miles J. Stanford. Copyright © 1975 by Miles J. Stanford. Used by permission of Zondervan Publishing House. Page 9.

WEEK 1, DAY 5
1. Kenneth S. Wuest, *Wuest's Word Studies of the Greek New Testament*, vol. 2 (Grand Rapids, Mich.: Eerdmans, 1973), p. 112.

WEEK 1, DAYS 6–7
1. G. Campbell Morgan, *Notes on the Psalms* (Tarrytown, N.Y.: Revell, 1947), p. 157. Used by permission.

WEEK 2, DAY 1
1. Thomas Watson, *The Godly Man's Picture* (Carlisle, Penn.: The Banner Of Truth Trust, 1992), p. 14.
2. Taken from *The Green Letters* by Miles J. Stanford. Copyright © 1975 by Miles J. Stanford. Used by permission of Zondervan Publishing House. Page 78.

WEEK 2, DAY 3
1. Arthur Bennett, *The Valley of Vision: A Collection of Puritan Prayers and Devotions* (Carlisle, Penn.: The Banner Of Truth Trust, 1975), p. 146. Used by permission.
2. Taken from *www.ccel.org*, citing Andrew Murray, *The Deeper Christian Life* (Fleming H. Revell, 1895).

WEEK 2, DAY 4
1. *Life Together* by Dietrich Bonhoeffer. English translation copyright © 1954 by Harper & Brothers; copyright renewed 1982 by Hellen S. Doberstein. San Francisco: HarperCollins. Pages 78-81. Used by permission.
2. Richard Weymouth, *New Testament in Modern Speech* (Grand Rapids, Mich.: Kregel Publications, 1978), p. 534.
3. Weymouth, p. 286.
4. From *F. B. Meyer Devotional Commentary* by F. B. Meyer.© 1989 by Tyndale House Publishers, Inc. Used by permission. All rights reserved. Page 564.

WEEK 2, DAY 5
1. Arthur Bennett, *The Valley of Vision: A Collection of Puritan Prayers and Devotions* (Carlisle, Penn.: The Banner Of Truth Trust, 1975), p. 108. Used by permission.
2. Derek Kidner, *Tyndale Old Testament Commentaries: Psalms 73–150* (Downers Grove, Ill.: InterVarsity, 1973), p. 307. Used by permission.

WEEK 2, DAYS 6–7

1. Charles Spurgeon, *The Treasury of David*, vol. 2 (McLean, Va.: MacDonald Publishing Company, n.d.), pp. 445-446.

WEEK 3, DAY 1

1. F. B. Meyer, *Choice Notes on the Psalms* (Grand Rapids, Mich.: Kregel Publications, 1984), p. 23.
2. Alan Redpath, *The Making of a Man of God* (Grand Rapids, Mich.: Baker Book House Company, 1962), p. 116. Used by permission.
3. Ronald Youngblood, *How It All Began* (Ventura, Calif.: Regal Books, 1980), p. 119.
4. Arthur Bennett, *The Valley of Vision: A Collection of Puritan Prayers and Devotions* (Carlisle, Penn.: The Banner Of Truth Trust, 1975), p. 75. Used by permission.
5. Mrs. Charles Cowman, *Streams in the Desert* (Los Angeles: The Oriental Missionary Society, 1925), pp. 44-46.
6. This material is taken from *Prayer: A Holy Occupation* by Oswald Chambers. Copyright ©1992 by the Oswald Chambers Publications Assoc., Ltd. Used by permission of Discovery House Publishers, Box 3566, Grand Rapids, MI 49501. All rights reserved. Page 150.

WEEK 3, DAY 2

1. Tony Lane, *The Lion Book of Christian Thought* (Oxford, England: Lion Publishing, 1984), p. 11.
2. This material is taken from *Prayer: A Holy Occupation* by Oswald Chambers. Copyright © 1992 by the Oswald Chambers Publications Assoc., Ltd. Used by permission of Discovery House Publishers, Box 3566, Grand Rapids, MI 49501. All rights reserved. Page 146.
3. Corrie ten Boom, *Each New Day* (Grand Rapids, Mich.: Revell, 1977), pp. 25, 89.

WEEK 3, DAY 3

1. Erwin W. Lutzer, *The Serpent of Paradise* (Chicago: Moody Press, 1996), pp. 119-120.
2. William Gurnall, *The Christian in Complete Armour*, vol. 1 (1655; reprint Carlisle, Penn.: The Banner Of Truth Trust, 1991), p. 34.

WEEK 3, DAY 4

1. Taken from *The Green Letters* by Miles J. Stanford. Copyright © 1975 by Miles J. Stanford. Used by permission of Zondervan Publishing House. Page 11.

WEEK 3, DAY 5

1. Taken from *More Than Conquerors* by John Woodbridge, ed., © 1992, Moody Bible Institute of Chicago. Moody Press. Used by permission. Pages 108-111.
2. S. Travena Jackson, *Fanny Crosby's Story of Ninety-Four Years* (New York: Fleming H. Revell, 1915), p. 28.
3. Janet Lindeblad Janzen with Richard J. Foster, *Songs for Renewal* (San Francisco: HarperCollins, 1995), p. xi.
4. This material is taken from *Christian Discipline* by Oswald Chambers. Copyright © 1935, 1936, 1995 by the Oswald Chambers Publications Assoc., Ltd. Originally published by Zondervan Publishers © 1985. Used by permission of Discovery House Publishers, Box 3566, Grand Rapids, MI 49501. All rights reserved. Page 56.

5. Amy Carmichael, *Gold by Moonlight* (Fort Washington, Penn.: Christian Literature Crusade, 1936), pp. 83-84. Used by permission.

WEEK 3, DAYS 6–7
1. James Montgomery Boice, *Psalms*, vol. 1 (Grand Rapids, Mich.: Baker Book House Company, 1994), pp. 111-112. Used by permission.

WEEK 4, DAY 1
1. Charles Spurgeon, *The Treasury of David*, vol. 1 (McLean, Va.: Macdonald Publishing Company, n.d.), pp. 339-340.

WEEK 4, DAY 3
1. J. I. Packer, *Knowing God* (Downers Grove, Ill.: InterVarsity, 1973, 1993), pp. 269-271. Used by permission.
2. Charles Spurgeon, *Morning and Evening* (Scotland: Christian Focus Publications, 1994), Aug. 31, morning.

WEEK 4, DAY 4
1. Tony Lane, *The Lion Book of Christian Thought* (Oxford, England: Lion Publishing, 1984), p. 127, and J. H. Merle D'Aubigne, *The Life and Times of Martin Luther* (Chicago: Moody, 1846).
2. James Montgomery Boice, *Psalms*, vol. 2 (Grand Rapids, Mich.: Baker Book House, 1996), pp. 687-693.
3. Dwight Hervey Small, *No Rival Love* (Fort Washington, Penn.: Christian Literature Crusade, 1984), pp. 37-38. Used by permission.
4. Charles Spurgeon, *Morning and Evening* (Scotland: Christian Focus Publications, 1994), July 19, morning.

WEEK 4, DAY 5
1. Arthur Bennett, *The Valley of Vision: A Collection of Puritan Prayers and Devotions* (Carlisle, Penn.: The Banner Of Truth Trust, 1975), p. 134. Used by permission.
2. Taken from *They Found the Secret* by V. Raymond Edman. Copyright © 1960 by Zondervan Publishing House. Used by permission of Zondervan Publishing House. Page 89.

WEEK 4, DAYS 6–7
1. G. Campbell Morgan, *Notes on the Psalms* (Tarrytown, N.Y.: Fleming H. Revell Company, 1947), pp. 88-89. Used by permission.

WEEK 5, DAY 1
1. Taken from *In the Footsteps of Jesus*. Copyright © 1997 by Bruce Marchiano. Published by Harvest House Publishers, Eugene, Oregon 97402 and Visual Entertainment, Dallas, Texas 75248. Used by permission. Page xi.
2. Basilea Schlink, *My All for Him* (Phoenix, Ariz.: Evangelical Sisterhood of Mary, 1971), pp. 23-25. Used by permission.
3. Charles Spurgeon, *Morning and Evening* (Scotland: Christian Focus Publications, 1994), May 22, evening.

Week 5, Day 2

1. Dr and Mrs. Howard Taylor, *Hudson Taylor's Spiritual Secret* (Chicago: Moody, 1989), p. 157.
2. Amy Carmichael, *Toward Jerusalem* (Fort Washington, Penn.: Christian Literature Crusade, 1936), p. 2. Used by permission.
3. Taken from *In the Footsteps of Jesus.* Copyright © 1997 by Bruce Marchiano. Published by Harvest House Publishers, Eugene, Oregon 97402 and Visual Entertainment, Dallas, Texas 75248. Used by permission. Page 133.

Week 5, Day 3

1. *Spiritual Disciplines for the Christian Life,* Donald S. Whitney, 1991. Used by permission of NavPress Publishing. All rights reserved. For copies of the book call 800-366-7788. Pages 175-176, 181.

Week 5, Day 4

1. Elisabeth Elliot, *Shadow of the Almighty* (San Francisco: Harper & Row, 1979), p. 38.
2. Elisabeth Elliot, *The Shadow of the Almighty* (San Francisco: Harper & Row, 1958), p. 15.
3. Quoted in David Hazard, *I Promise You a Crown* (Minneapolis, Minn.: Bethany House Publishers, 1995), p. 47. Used by permission.

Week 5, Day 5

1. From *www.eric-liddell.org;* Kate Maxwell, a review of *Complete Surrender* by Julian Wilson.
2. *The Complete Word Study Dictionary,* compiled and edited by Spiros Zodhiates, AMG Publishers, Chattanooga, Tenn., 1992. Page 937. Used by permission.
3. From the book *The Pursuit of God* by A. W. Tozer. Copyright 1982, 1993 by Christian Publications, Inc., Camp Hill, Penn. Used with permission. Page 27.
4. From *The Pursuit of God,* pp. 30-31. Used with permission.

Week 5, Days 6–7

1. Matthew Henry, *Matthew Henry's Commentary* (Grand Rapids, Mich.: Zondervan, 1961), p. 583.
2. *Life Application® Bible* © 1988, 1989, 1990, 1991 by Tyndale House Publishers, Inc., Wheaton, IL 60189. All rights reserved. Life Application is a registered trademark of Tyndale House Publishers, Inc. Page 904.
3. James Montgomery Boice, *Psalms,* vol. 1 (Grand Rapids, Mich.: Baker Book House Company, 1994), p. 46. Used by permission.

Week 6, Day 1

1. Reprinted from *Daily Prayers.* Copyright © 1995 by Harold Shaw Publishers. WaterBrook Press, Colorado Springs, CO. All rights reserved. Page 16.
2. A. W. Tozer, *The Knowledge of the Holy, the Attributes of God: Their Meaning in the Christian Life* (San Francisco: HarperCollins, 1992), pp. 129, 159.
3. *Man of Prayer,* Frank C. Laubach, © 1990, New Readers Press, U.S. Publishing Division of Laubach Literacy, used by permission. Pages 195-196.

WEEK 6, DAY 2
1. Excerpted from Lyle Wesley Dorsett, *E. M. Bounds: Man of Prayer* (Grand Rapids, Mich.: Zondervan, 1991), pp. 138-139. Used by permission.
2. From the book *The Pursuit of God* by A. W. Tozer. Copyright 1982, 1993 by Christian Publications, Inc., Camp Hill, Penn. Used with permission. Page 12.
3. Richard Foster, *Prayer: Finding the Heart's True Home* (San Francisco: HarperCollins, 1992), pp. 3-4.
4. John Bunyan, *Prayer* (1662; reprint Carlisle, Penn.: The Banner Of Truth Trust, 1995), p. 19.
5. Reprinted from *Prayer* by O. Hallesby, copyright © 1931, 1959 Augsburg Publishing House. Used by permission of Augsburg Fortress. Pages 11-13.

WEEK 6, DAY 3
1. Lyle Wesley Dorsett, *E. M. Bounds: Man of Prayer* (Grand Rapids, Mich.: Zondervan, 1991), p. 26. Used by permission.
2. Arthur Bennett, *The Valley of Vision: A Collection of Puritan Prayers and Devotions* (Carlisle, Penn.: The Banner Of Truth Trust, 1975), p. 130. Used by permission.
3. Reprinted from *Prayer* by O. Hallesby, copyright © 1931, 1959 Augsburg Publishing House. Used by permission of Augsburg Fortress. Pages 21, 26.
4. E. M. Bounds, *The Necessity of Prayer* (Grand Rapids, Mich.: Baker Book House, 1976), p. 14.

WEEK 6, DAY 4
1. Lyle Wesley Dorsett, *E. M. Bounds: Man of Prayer* (Grand Rapids, Mich.: Zondervan, 1991), page 58. Used by permission.
2. Taken from *God's Best Secrets* by Andrew Murray. Copyright 1993, Kregel Publications, Grand Rapids, MI. Used by permission. Page 18.
3. Judson Cornwall, *Praying the Scriptures* (Lake Mary, Fla.: Creation House, 1988), p. 49. Used by permission.
4. D.A. Carson, *A Call to Spiritual Reformation* (Grand Rapids, Mich.: Baker Book House, 1992), pp. 20-22. Used by permission.

WEEK 6, DAY 5
1. This story was found at various websites on the Internet.
2. John F. Walvoord and Roy B. Zuck, eds., *The Bible Knowledge Commentary: Old Testament* (Wheaton, Ill.: Victor Books, 1985), pp. 1250-1251, and Frank E. Gaebelein, ed., *The Expositor's Bible Commentary*, vol. 6 (Grand Rapids, Mich.: Zondervan, 1986), pp. 799-803.
3. Excerpted from Jennifer Kennedy Dean, *The Praying Life: Living Beyond Your Limits* (Birmingham, Ala.: New Hope Publishers, © 1994). All rights reserved. Used by permission. Pages 9-18.
4. Alice Smith, *Beyond the Veil* (Ventura, Calif.: Regal Books, 1997), p. 34. Used by permission.
5. This material is taken from *Prayer: A Holy Occupation* by Oswald Chambers. Copyright © 1992 by the Oswald Chambers Publications Assoc., Ltd. Used by permission of Discovery House Publishers, Box 3566, Grand Rapids, MI 49501. All rights reserved. Page 130.
6. Reprinted from *Daily Prayers*. Copyright © 1995 by Harold Shaw Publishers. WaterBrook Press, Colorado Springs, CO. All rights reserved. Page 131.

WEEK 6, DAYS 6–7

1. From *F. B. Meyer Devotional Commentary* by F. B. Meyer.© 1989 by Tyndale House Publishers, Inc. Used by permission. All rights reserved. Page 264.

WEEK 7, DAY 1

1. Alan Redpath, *The Making of a Man of God* (Grand Rapids, Mich.: Baker Book House Company, 1962), p. 5. Used by permission.
2. Catherine Marshall, ed., *The Prayers of Peter Marshall* (Grand Rapids, Mich.: Fleming H. Revell, a division of Baker Book House Company, 1982), p. 113. Used by permission.
3. Copyrighted 1979, by Bill Bright, *NewLife* Publications, Campus Crusade for Christ. All rights reserved. Used by permission. Page 1.
4. Charles Spurgeon, *Morning and Evening* (Scotland: Christian Focus Publications, 1994), March 7, morning.
5. From the book *The Pursuit of God* by A. W. Tozer. Copyright 1982, 1993 by Christian Publications, Inc., Camp Hill, Penn. Used with permission. Page 138.

WEEK 7, DAY 2

1. *The Complete Word Study Dictionary*, compiled and edited by Spiros Zodhiates, AMG Publishers, Chattanooga, Tenn., 1992. Page 1162. Used by permission.
2. Kenneth S. Wuest, *Wuest's Word Studies of the Greek New Testament*, vol. 2 (Grand Rapids, Mich.: Eerdmans, 1973), p. 193. Used by permission.
3. From the book *The Pursuit of God* by A. W. Tozer. Copyright 1982, 1993 by Christian Publications, Inc., Camp Hill, Penn. Used with permission. Pages 138-139.
4. Ney Bailey, *Faith Is Not a Feeling* (Bloomington, Ind.: Integrated Resources, 1978), pp. 24-25. Used by permission.
5. Marie Henry, *The Secret Life of Hannah Whitall Smith* (Minneapolis, Minn.: Bethany House, 1993), p. 105. Used by permission.
6. This material is taken from *My Utmost for His Highest* by Oswald Chambers. Copyright © 1935 by Dodd Mead & Co., renewed © 1963 by the Oswald Chambers Publications Assn., Ltd., and is used by permission of Discovery House Publishers, Box 3566, Grand Rapids, MI 49501. All rights reserved. Page 304.

WEEK 7, DAY 3

1. First published in *The Olney Hymns*, bk. 3, no. 48, in a section of hymns entitled "Comfort." The original of *The Olney Hymns* comprised three books bound into one volume, and has a preface dated February 15, 1779, by Cowper's friend John Newton (ex–slave trader). Much thanks to George Davies, trustee, Cowper and Newton Museum in Olney, Bucks, U.K., for information about this hymn.
2. This material is taken from *My Utmost for His Highest* by Oswald Chambers. Copyright © 1935 by Dodd Mead & Co., renewed © 1963 by the Oswald Chambers Publications Assn., Ltd., and is used by permission of Discovery House Publishers, Box 3566, Grand Rapids, MI 49501. All rights reserved. Page 305.

3. Mrs. Charles Cowman, *Streams in the Desert* (Los Angeles: The Oriental Missionary Society, 1925), p. 5.

Week 7, Day 4

1. A. W. Tozer, *The Knowledge of the Holy, the Attributes of God: Their Meaning in the Christian Life* (San Francisco: HarperCollins, 1992), pp. v2-v2i.
2. Copyrighted 1979, by Bill Bright, *NewLife* Publications, Campus Crusade for Christ. All rights reserved. Used by permission. Page 1.

Week 7, Day 5

1. Reprinted from *Daily Prayers*. Copyright © 1995 by Harold Shaw Publishers. WaterBrook Press, Colorado Springs, CO. All rights reserved. Page 8.

Week 7, Days 6–7

1. F. B. Meyer, *Choice Notes on the Psalms* (Grand Rapids, Mich.: Kregel Publications, 1984), p. 91.

Week 8, Day 1

1. Taken from *Theological Wordbook of the Old Testament: Volume 2* by R. Laird Harris, ed., copyright © 1980, Moody Bible Institute of Chicago. Moody Press. Used by permission. Page 210.
2. Robert Baker Girdlestone, *Synonyms of the Old Testament* (Grand Rapids, Mich.: Baker Book House Company, 1983), p. 51. Used by permission.
3. Nathan Stone, *Names of God* (Chicago: Moody, 1944), p. 25.
4. Alan Redpath, *The Making of a Man of God* (Grand Rapids, Mich.: Baker Book House Company, 1962), pp. 91-92. Used by permission.

Week 8, Day 2

1. Doug Hartman and Doug Sutherland, *A Guidebook to Discipleship* (Irvine, Calif.: Harvest House, 1976), p. 31.
2. Debra Collins, © August 1999. Used by permission.
3. Amy Carmichael, *Toward Jerusalem* (Fort Washington, Penn.: Christian Literature Crusade, 1936), p. 116. Used by permission.
4. Robert Coleman, *The Master Plan of Evangelism* (Grand Rapids, Mich.: Fleming H. Revell, a division of Baker Book House Company, 1974), p. 18. Used by permission.

Week 8, Day 3

1. Elisabeth Elliot, *A Chance to Die* (Grand Rapids, Mich.: Fleming H. Revell, a division of Baker Book House Company, 1987), p. 84. Used by permission.
2. Elliot, p. 16. Used by permission.
3. Amy Carmichael, *Toward Jerusalem* (Fort Washington, Penn.: Christian Literature Crusade, 1936), p. 94. Used by permission.
4. Ann Kiemel Anderson, *Yes* (Wheaton, Ill.: Tyndale House, 1978), p. 12. Used by permission. For the story of John and Betty Stam, see *The Triumph of John and Betty Stam* by Mrs. Howard Taylor.
5. A. B. Bruce, *The Training of the Twelve* (Grand Rapids, Mich.: Kregel Publications, 1971), pp. 12-13.

6. Anderson, p. 12. Used by permission.

7. Anderson, p. 10. Used by permission.

WEEK 8, DAY 4

1. A. B. Bruce, *The Training of the Twelve* (Grand Rapids, Mich.: Kregel Publications, 1971), pp. 44, 49.

2. From the sermon "Heaven Below" taken from *Spurgeon's Sermons*, vol. 15 (New York: Funk & Wagnalls, 1884), pp. 205-206.

3. Taken from the sermon "Hid with Christ" by Gypsy Smith in *As Jesus Passed By* (New York, Toronto: Fleming H. Revell, 1905), p. 194.

WEEK 8, DAY 5

1. Taken from *Theological Wordbook of the Old Testament: Volume 2* by R. Laird Harris, ed., copyright © 1980, Moody Bible Institute of Chicago. Moody Press. Used by permission. Page 791.

2. Brennan Manning, *The Signature of Jesus* (Sisters, Ore.: Questar Publishers, 1996), pp. 31-32. Used by permission of the author.

about the author

CATHERINE MARTIN is a summa cum laude graduate of Bethel Theological Seminary with a Master of Arts in Theological Studies. She is founder and president of Quiet Time Ministries and is dedicated to teaching devotion to God and His Word. She also serves as director of women's ministries at a large church in Southern California and as adjunct faculty at Biola University. Teaching at retreats and conferences, she challenges others to seek God and love Him with all of their heart, soul, mind, and strength.

Other books in the Quiet Times for the Heart Series.

Revive My Heart!

ISBN-13: 978-1-57683-379-7
ISBN-10: 1-57683-379-8

Studying passages such as Psalm 119, this book looks at many aspectsof personal spiritual revival. Through this you can gain spiritual depth, joy, and access to your heavenly Father's resources in times of trouble.

A Heart That Dances

ISBN-13: 978-1-57683-380-3
ISBN-10: 1-57683-380-1

This journey of daily quiet times will help you learn how several biblical characters interacted with God and how to apply that knowledge to your life.

To order copies, visit your local Christian bookstore, call NavPress at
1-800-366-7788, or log on to www.navpress.com.
To locate a Christian bookstore near you, call 1-800-991-7747.